I am Porcelain

The Naked Truth Vol. 2

BRITTINY D. MOREHEAD

I am Porcelain

This is a work created based on real-life events in which are portrayed to the best of Brittiny D. Morehead's memory. All encounters of said events are true, no names have been mentioned to protect the privacy of all parties involved. No characters have been conjured up and no events were fabricated.

I am Porcelain, The Naked Truth Vol. 2

Copyright © 2020 by Brittiny D. Morehead

All rights reserved. No part of this book may be reproduced or used in any manner without written permission of the copyright owner except for the use of quotations in a book review.

Printed in the United States of America

First Printing, 2020

ISBN-13: 978-1-7357901-0-7 (8.5 x 11 in Paperback)

ISBN-13: 978-1-7357901-1-4 (E-book)

ISBN-13: 978-1-7357901-2-1 (6 x 9 in Paperback)

ISBN-13: 978-1-7357901-3-8 (6 x 9 in Hardcover)

The first edition of this book was printed in 2014

ISBN-13: 978-1500234164

ISBN-10: 1500234168

Front cover image by Keith Hepinstall/Keith Hepinstall Digital Art and Photography

Photographs of Brittiny D. Morehead by William Washington/Extreme Works Studio

Published by Eat My Lyrics Publishing Company, LLC

https://brittinydmorehead.com

I am Porcelain

Have You Met Your Author Lately?

Brittiny D. Morehead, Author of The Naked Truth and I am Porcelain, was born August 3, 1991, in Fort Worth, Texas.

Brittiny discovered the magic behind words very early in her childhood, where lots of sadness, drunken rage, and arguing took place. She couldn't fathom the reality of being in a family that seemed to be so dysfunctional; writing carried her away from it all.

Brittiny was a fatherless child who grew up with 8 of 11 siblings. Surrounded by so many kids, she wanted something of her own, someone even; so, she chose to accommodate her desires for attention by learning the art of sex. She became infatuated with boys because they made her feel that she mattered. With boys came sex, with sex came love, and with love came rape, a miscarriage, STDs, and growing up entirely too fast; but through it all, there was writing and there was poetry.

Brittiny attended Eastern Hills High School, where she became President of a well-known organization that worked with distressed and disruptive teenagers; UMOJA. She won a poetry competition associated with this program and was inspired to continue to utilize her voice.

Brittiny was thankful that she could heal from and overcome her experiences, but she couldn't quite let them all go, so she launched her first poetic novel, The Naked Truth in July of 2014; where she also experienced the loss of her mother only 10 days later. She realized that she was nothing without the passion behind her words, so while grieving, she used her pain and tears as fuel to add to the fire that already burned inside her.

The Naked Truth, described to be "Maya Angelou meets Zane," sold out in less than two hours at its first book signing, located at a local Walmart.

Brittiny D. Morehead is also a Spoken Word Artist, Public Speaker, Ghostwriter, Publisher and Article Writer. She continues to write so that she may uplift, empower, and inspire broken daughters all around the world, in which suffer the same realities that she once did.

Brittiny advocates for the voices that are too afraid to speak, and she acknowledges that she is able to articulate the meaning of the power behind words.

I am Porcelain

Let's Get Social; Stay Connected

FACEBOOK:
Author Brittiny D. Morehead (ADD ME)

FACEBOOK LIKE PAGE #1:
Author Brittiny D. Morehead (PLEASE LIKE)

FACEBOOK LIKE PAGE #2:
I am Porcelain, The Naked Truth Vol. 2 (PLEASE LIKE)

TWITTER:
@TalkThatShit_B (FOLLOW ME)

INSTAGRAM:
@TalkThatShitBritt (FOLLOW ME)

LINKEDIN:
Author Brittiny D. Morehead (CONNECT)

YOUTUBE CHANNEL:
Talk That Shit Britt (SUBSCRIBE)

WORDPRESS:
TalkThatShitBritt (SUBSCRIBE)

I am Porcelain: The Naked Truth

The poetic novel that will change your life.

iBleedPoetry

I am Porcelain

Contents

A Letter for My Broken Daughters	13-14
Dedications	15-16
Intro	17

WARNING

For Display Only	19-36
Forgive Me Father, For I have Sinned	38-53
Invested Afflictions	55-77
Naked	79-97
Tainted Hearts	99-113
Reflections	114

FAN FAVORITES

1. *I Had my Husband's Mistress*	117-122
2. *BITCH was the title that they gave me*	123-127
3. *For My Mother*	128-131
4. *Favors*	132-134
5. *Slavery in Reverse*	135-140

THEY LIED TO YOU

6. *Betrayal at its Best*	143-146

7.	Never	147-150
8.	You	151
9.	You Said	152
10.	Why Does He?	153
11.	Reflections of my Past	154
12.	Fifty Shades of Fucked Up	155- 156
13.	Mistaken	157
14.	November	158- 160
15.	Sleepless Nights	161- 162
16.	Mommy Loves You	163- 165
17.	Separations of Darkness	166- 170
18.	Fatherless Child	171- 174
19.	Why Does the Bruises of a Lover's Fist?	175- 179
20.	The Real Shit	180- 182
21.	The Kiss of Death	183-184
22.	In Pain, I've Changed, & Now, I've Overcame	185- 187
23.	I Just Wish I knew	188- 189
24.	Eternal Bruises	190- 191
25.	Crying Pains	192- 193
26.	Church	194- 196
27.	It's been years	197- 199
28.	Help Me	200- 201
29.	Can you save me?	202-203
30.	Bruises of a Lover's Fist	204

I am Porcelain

31.	Self-Inflicted Wounds	205-207
32.	Corruption	208-209
33.	My Existence	210
34.	I'll never clock out of life	211-212
35.	Daddy's Little Girl's Confession	213-217
36.	Jasmine Mans	218-225
37.	Flawless Perceptions	226-227
38.	I Control You	228
39.	Gay Pride	229-237
40.	A flow of confusion	238-239
41.	A Book & its Cover	240-241
42.	I Quit	242-243
43.	Breaking Away	244
44.	The Disappearance	245-246
45.	Unpredictable	247-248
46.	We're the Same	249-250
47.	Forbidden Love	251-253
48.	Love like This	252-255
49.	Her	256-257
50.	Want Me	258-261
51.	Sex w/ You	262-264
52.	My Dove	265-267
53.	Confrontations w/ the Dove	268-269
54.	Dreaming of your Kiss	270

I am Porcelain

55. Those Eyes	271
56. Love	272-273
57. Love is	274
58. Love Affair	275-277
59. Marry Me	278
60. Making Love	279-280
61. Happy Valentine's Day	281
Fatherless Child; A Change Gone Come	283-285

SOME WORDS FOR YOU

62. Better	287-290
63. Fire in the Sky	291-292
64. Somebody Else	293-296
65. AWE	297-298
66. She lost her P	299-300
67. When I Die	301
68. Reminiscence	302
69. Angry	303
70. Dreaming	304
71. Does it rain in the Summer?	305-306
72. Tyler Perry	307-308
73. Tainted	309-310
74. MAMA	311
75. Empty Flying Bullets	312-313

I am Porcelain

76. My First Love	314- 315
77. PAIN	316- 217
78. Broken Memories	318- 321
79. The Stutter of a Broken Child	322- 323
80. The Ramblings of a Broken Woman	324- 325
81. Who am I?	326
82. Face Destroyed	327- 329
83. WOMAN	330- 331
84. A Missed Call	332- 333
85. More Truth	334
86. Manipulations of the Heart	335- 336
87. Baby Boy; The Poem	337- 339
88. Stand	340
89. Gun Violence	341
90. Freedom	342
91. Jesus Wept, & So Did I	343- 344
92. Dear Mama	345- 346
93. Ghetto	347- 348
94. I'm So Dope	349- 351
95. Well Played	352- 353
96. When THEY see US	354- 355
97. Gifts	356
98. I'm No Mother	357- 358
99. Beauty	359

I am Porcelain

100.	ATTENTION	360
101.	*Judge Me Not*	361
102.	*She Swallows*	362-363
103.	*Withered*	364
104.	*Something about the way she ate my pussy*	365-366
105.	*For the Big Girls*	367-369
106.	*Green Boxes*	370-371
107.	*Free my Pussy*	372-373
108.	BIG	374-375
109.	*You a Poet?*	376-378

One More Story — 380-387

The Naked Truth -Version 1 — 389-390

Reviews from Amazon — 391-392

Reviews from Social Media — 393-400

Wise Words from Me to You — 401-407

Motivation — 408-410

What's Next? — 411

Farewell — 412

Reflections — 413-415

I am Porcelain

A Letter for my Broken Daughters

  I was sitting at a table one day after what seemed to be the roughest conversation that I've ever had about myself. I realized that I was more than just some mentally warped person, I was a broken daughter. I then wondered if someone took the time out to leave a letter or two for me. After battling with voices in my head, I began to write…

  We do not come about being damaged, disturbed, or scorned for no reason. We are slaves to our pasts; we feel that we must submit and conform to what we're used to. This is not so. I learned that once we finally let go, we grow. Do not let a man or woman ~~take your life away~~ without taking your life away.

  We as women must know that we are powerful and that our lives hold weight. We do not need mankind to determine our worth. When was the last time you loved yourself properly? Did you feel pretty? Did you melt at the glance of your own face? No? Well honey, you're not trying hard enough. You ARE attractive. You ARE breathtaking. You ARE sexy. Empower yourself because if you lean on another human to do it, you have failed already.

  I waited to be validated and believed in, which was

my first mistake. I thought that if I gave myself away enough to people who may or may not matter, then they'd give me what I wanted- second mistake.

What did I want? Everything. What did I give away? Everything. What did I truly receive? A body count, STDs, judgement, weight gain, failed engagements, and disappointment. My father's nonexistence contributed to the rise of my rebellion, but he was only one of the many screws that I was missing.

We are all improperly assembled, but it's okay because the fun is in putting ourselves back together. So, don't judge yourself, love yourself.

Sincerely,
B

I am Porcelain

Dedications

To my family, fans, and friends, I created this masterpiece for you because you embrace the art of my pain through the essence of my words. To the broken daughters, the broken women, I dedicate my truths to you. For we have suffered this life in a way that no one could ever imagine.

To my grandmother, I thank you for raising me with unconditional love; you've shown me forgiveness and strength in myself. You are the light that I will always need. Thank you for allowing me to bury my soul on paper while growing up, it was the beginning of my forever. Dad, I thank you for returning to me a man of honesty and of protection; it's what I've always wanted. You too have shown me the art of forgiveness, I love you dearly. Mom, I hate that you missed who you inspired me to become. I learned how to dream from you. You will forever be the life of my party. Granddad, thank you for loving me beyond your battles with cancer, you've shown me GOD is good even when you're bad.

To my bonus mothers, you all were present in different seasons of my life, but I value you forever. I thank you for being part of the village that raised me. Your encouragement and belief in me proved that I was and am supposed to be somebody. To my dear siblings, cousins, and aunties, I thank you all for the living room and parking lot sessions of listening to my poetry; after so long, I finally feel heard. You all are the glue to my madness.

To my partner, I thank you for showing me that women ought to think more highly of themselves. You've taught me balance between my past and my future. I thank you for understanding that even I am human. Without your love, I would've sunken into a different type of destruction. You've shown me purity, and that is why I dedicate my growth to you.

To my real friends, YOU are the turn up that I've needed every step of the way! I thank you all for reading snippets of my book, crying with me, laughing with me, and celebrating ME in defining moments of my life. You're the support system that I never had.

And to all supporters unknown, I thank you for facing my truths with me.

Intro

Poetry is more than just a line of beautiful words.

Poetry is pain on a Friday night.

It's love, on a Monday morning.

It's miscarriages in April and nightmares in November;

Poetry is healing.

Poetry is voices that have never been heard, and it's far more than I could ever explain, but as I continue to relay my realities, and my deepest darkest secrets, I hope to see you there.

Welcome to The Naked Truth.

I am Porcelain

I am Porcelain; The Naked Truth

A Slave to my Past.

I am Porcelain

For Display Only

During my years as an elementary school student, my class was given a project utilizing *pottery*. We were instructed to create something special for Mother's Day. I hadn't quite encountered this type of clay before, it was weird and wet; I did the best that I could to mold the unusual clump into a beauty. From what I recall, it went through a process and upon completion; it dried and turned out to be very smooth, colorful, and solid. It was in the shape of a bowl and although it was solid, I found out very quickly that I had to handle it with care. I took the item home and gifted it to my mother, she of course, loved it. It sat for a while and then eventually, it became an ashtray for her habit. As time moved along, it was dropped repeatedly, therefore it was constantly breaking off; chipping apart. I remember being a little disappointed because all I knew was there would one day be no more pottery, no more ashtray, no more clay, and I was right.

I then began to grow an attachment to these types of dolls that I'd see in my grandmother's magazines. I always inquired about them because they appeared to be much different than the ordinary Barbie Doll, *in which I was no*

I am Porcelain

fan of playing with. Every time I asked about them, I was told that they too had to be handled with care and that they were not meant to be toys; they were *"made for show,"* because they were porcelain dolls. My curiosity began; I didn't understand why they were for display only. My grandmother would say, *"one wrong move and they will shatter."* I was in awe. What did that even mean? Dolls shatter? What doll isn't to be played with? Talk about being bewildered.

I had witnessed the breaking of many nice plates prior to this discovery, but I was so amazed at the delicacy of something so beautiful, and how it could be this fragile. My grandmother went on to say *"Brittiny, you know them thangs break"* but I didn't, I just knew that they were pretty. I unknowingly began to take form to this newfound doll, both inside and out; unique.

I observed my mother a lot while growing up. I admired the very many ways in which she enjoyed her life; she was absolutely wild, courageous, attractive, and carefree. Her passion for hair and beauty led her to becoming a very well-known cosmetologist in the community. Although her clientele was consistent, she always made time to "doll us up" too. Eventually, I wanted my hair to be

I am Porcelain

longer, so I asked for extensions. After being able to wear a nice length, I wanted to keep taking it up a notch. At this point, she was not happy styling my hair weekly, so I learned how to style my own hair; Needless to say, I mastered this. I enjoyed feeling glamourous every day; the hair, nails/toes, makeup, and clothes, *had I become for display only*?

I was in Jr. high when I went out on a limb and begged my mother for red hair, she said yes. Red was very vibrant, bold, and loud; everyone loved it, so I gave them more, just like my mother did. From Kim's clothing to her hair, she turned heads everywhere she went. Imagine a model coming up to your school who just so happened to be your mother, the attention that she received was so overwhelming. My sisters and I obsessively heard how "fine" our mother was from boyfriends, teachers, and friends. She was in fact drop dead gorgeous and absolutely stunning; I wanted to be just like her. I needed to be just like her. I had to be. I looked for more ways to alter my appearance so that I didn't feel average; being average was an insult to me. I changed my wardrobe and would even sneak and wear my mother's clothes because they looked sexy on me. I wanted to be the girl that guys would break their necks to have.

I am Porcelain

    Men started chasing me at this point and although I knew that they chased all girls my age, it didn't stop me from entertaining them. I dated guys here and there, so I began to pay attention to their preferences. I subconsciously mimicked what I found the epitome of pretty to be until I found myself- by myself again. I was always different. I wore jewelry in my hair and extensions that were longer than what was depicted to be okay. I remember walking to one of my classes as a group of girls lingered behind me. One of the them uttered "Now she knows that is NOT her hair" prior to bursting into laughter with her hyenas. I walked with my head high, allowing those eighteen inches to sway right above the crack of my ass; unbothered. Luckily, I didn't live for the approval of others. Days like this empowered me because I felt as though I were in demand. Often, I'd be just the bitch to tell them that their boyfriends or their daddies liked it.

    I was laughed at for stepping outside of the box but when I tuned in to my environment, I saw more and more girls doing the same damn thing, how about that?! I was teased for the way that I wore my makeup, not having name brand shoes, and for being different. I grew so tired of encounters with "mean girls" that I too became one. I didn't know this at the time but reflecting on it now, that's exactly what happened. I flaunted my victories in the best ways that I could; in their faces. I stole boyfriends, strung along their crushes, and berated them in front of others; I became ruthless. Little did I know, I was tampering with who I could've been.

I opened the door to possess dysfunctional qualities but aside from devious behaviors, I was very wild, free spirited, and daring. I did whatever I wanted to do, hell sometimes whomever I wanted to do. I made plenty of friends, several enemies, and I tried my best to move forward so that I could embark on something new, love.

Relationships became a playground for me; I was always seeing someone different. Due to my inability to adapt to bullshit, I found myself dismissing guys left and right, even though I found happiness with them all. My mother became concerned but couldn't quite communicate her concerns correctly; she ended up lashing out at me one day. I recall her yelling *"I don't want you to be some hoe,"* as I darted the door to meet my 21-year-old male friend whom awaited me downstairs. I was in fact sexually active, but not with him. She didn't know that. I was 16 years old and as I stated, he was 21. He and I became acquainted because we worked together. This guy was Caucasian and drove a Crown Victoria on twenty-two-inch rims; he was all the hood a girl could ask for. I was very uneasy about the difference in our color, but I ignored it because I really liked him. We simply got to know one another. He respected me, was present whenever I needed him, and fawned over me as if I were the most royal Queen there could ever be. I didn't have to open my legs, hands, or mouth for this treatment. I couldn't let him get away because he was different.

I grew up in mostly a two-bedroom apartment with several siblings. I wanted attention, a lot of it. This guy gave me his undivided attention, transported me to and from work, and made himself available to me always; I was inevitably taken by his efforts of appealing to me. Our relationship began rocky because of the age difference but eventually he was accepted by my mother and my grandmother, so all was well in my world... right? Not so much. I had taken on something that I hadn't quite prepared myself for; interracial dating. Interracial dating is when you date someone of a different ethnicity or race than you. I didn't see color before now, so what was the big deal?

We became serious but this was still not a sexual relationship, believe it or not. We still wanted to respect the boundaries of our ages, reflecting now, I truly appreciate that. We met each other's families and eventually went public; this is where things became difficult. We interacted as a normal couple; he picked me up from school, work, and took me out to spend time with me. I say that things became difficult because I didn't know that being involved with him would lead to the depleting of my confidence. One of the most embarrassing times that I can remember is being at the mall with him and running into classmates from my high school. I wasn't the most popular, but a lot of people knew me, I was *"Elmo."* So, any who, he and I were holding hands and walking through the mall when I heard, "ELMO, YOU GO WITH A WHITE BOY?! Man, you don't know what to do with no black girl!" -I was mortified. We were subjected to rude comments and stares because of what we looked like with one another; ridiculous I presume. I tried to shake it off by holding onto his hand tighter, while shaking my head as if I didn't care. I didn't care that anyone knew we were together, but I cared that it projected so many negative vibes and that our being together put us in so many awkward situations.

A ride home from work to a local park set the tone for my being reluctant to our relationship. We were at a park located near our job because we had just gotten off, so we were tired and just wanted to decompress. I guess the police

I am Porcelain

officer, which happened to be white, thought otherwise. Initially, she approached us about the park having a curfew and then very quickly, things escalated to her accusing me of having a chip on my shoulder, ha. Funny how the only "chip" that I had, involved her judging the nature of our relationship.

Being that I am now 28 years old, I can see how I may have appeared to be just some fast-tale, 16-year-old girl with a grown ass man. I can't be too upset that she judged me there, but the residue that lingered took me for an emotional ride, as did she. The officer instructed him to exit the location so that she could escort me home, because of my age. The ride home was so uncomfortable; I rode in the back of the damn cop car and she continued to talk to me as if I weren't even worth the stare, - I was pissed. When we arrived at my grandmother's home, the cop let me out and as I marched through the door, I could hear her speaking with my grandmother about my age, my boyfriend, and her perception. My grandmother heard her out and eventually spoke with me about it but as I stated before, I was open about this relationship with her and my mother because of how delicate the truth was; I was too young. Not only was I too young, I was now insecure. I didn't know if I wished for him to be black or for me to be white. I dwelled on the thought of myself being white or him being with someone of his own race, it was overwhelming. I began to obsess about it until I finally just asked him why he was with ME. He gave me a very nice and honest answer, in which put me at ease for a while, but being insecure doesn't vanish overnight. The relationship was over before it started but we stayed in contact and remained good friends.

As life moved along for me, I pressed forward doing what I did best, encountering another story to tell. I am no therapist or counselor but in courses related to this field, we are first taught the essence of our common sense. My common sense now tells me that my lack of having a father mangled my potential and encouraged my promiscuity. Now some of you may read this and assume that this should've been apparent to me before, but to know me is to know that I am stubborn; I did not want to accept that I was a stereotype. I didn't want to give my father's absence that much credit, but facts are facts. I needed him and all I wanted was for him to need me too. However, I was dealt a different batch of cards.

I was one of the oldest of many children, and I had plenty of time to find trouble with my former child-hood friend who carried the same first name as I. We had so much

I am Porcelain

in common; We both played the clarinet and had last names that began with the letter M. We loved various types of music and could do just about anything we wanted. At the age of 12, one night at her house changed my life; I lost my virginity. It was the summer before my 13th birthday, what the hell was I thinking right? Well to be honest, it wasn't my intent for this to happen. You know back then "hunching" was the thing to do. That's all it was supposed to be, even when he utilized his tool to jab at my underwear. Boy was I stupid; I found out what being "wet" was that day. There was a slippery slope in-between my legs and my mind; his penis didn't fail to miss the target. With no hands at all, it just slid in my vagina, stabbing through the side of my panties. I was in shock, I clenched tightly and gasped, but I allowed it to just happen. From this experience, I became EXTREMELY sexually active. I couldn't live without it.

When you sign yourself up for sex, you are contracted to cause turmoil in your life because with sex comes STDs, pregnancies/miscarriages, love, rape, betrayal, heartache, and pain. With sex comes a lot of shit that you cannot change, it is something that should be taken seriously. However, we live in a generation that thrives off of sex and after losing my virginity, that's all that I could do too.

I am Porcelain

I endured so much by utilizing my body for a sex toy. I sit back now, and I just contemplate so many things that I could have and should have done differently… but then I realize, I wouldn't have anything to tell if I altered those moments, now would I?

Life is a rude motherfucker dressed in sunshine, instilled to break us down and build us back up, as we come to terms with who we are. A lot of us don't get to make it through but I tell you this, you may have screwed Tom, Dick, Harry, Peter, Paul, and Frank, but baby you are the bomb! I don't care what you did, how you did it, or who you did it with; you are worthy of love and respect! We were meant to be loved in all the wrong ways so that we could come together and find our true light.

We are those dolls, built fragilely in order to convey the sharpness of our beauty, the delicacy of our skin, and the holes in the spaces of where our hearts should be. We are this generations' Broken Daughters.

Being in a big family is fun but it can also be challenging, especially when you're faced with comparisons to your siblings. I grew up with three brothers and five sisters, one in which is my fraternal twin. We looked alike growing up but as we grew older, we began to form identities

I am Porcelain

of our own. We were compared to one another by everyone around us and even though my twin sister loved me to death and would die to protect me, I feel as though their comparisons hung our relationship. There was an invisible noose, tightening on the throat of us every time someone called me the prettier twin, the better singer, or the better dancer. I would be delighted for any compliment but ones insulting her and elevating me, made me cringe inside sometimes. We never spoke about it because we were just kids, but all I could think about is how she must've felt, and if she hated *me* for what *they* thought. My twin was always very confident in herself, still is, but it sucks to be compared to another girl, especially your own sister. She never indicated any hurt behind those comments, we just slowly drifted away from one another.

A lot began to surface as we became adults, but I felt that it was just common drama for dysfunctional families; I was convinced that everybody had one. Ironically now, I am being compared to her. I'm pressured to be more like her. I hear how she's domestic, hard-working, and family oriented. I have never been the one to fit those shoes. She loves to cook, clean, and take care of home. I commend her for all the qualities in which make her an amazing mother and wife, but none of those things represent me.

Since this book is about my *Naked Truth,* I will admit that I cannot cook and do not want to, I rarely clean but if I do, I must be drinking and have my music playing, and I am not family oriented (I hate Chuck E Cheese with a passion and any place similar to it). I simply live for adult fun (anything that involves alcohol and sex), it's oddly embedded in me. Luckily, my partner loves to cook, clean, and orchestrate family friendly fun, she knows that the highlight of those functions must involve liquor for me. I feel as though these traits stem from Kim, I am truly my mother's child. God rest her soul.

In my adult years, I've felt torn down internally when my twin and I are together; she's praised for being married and having such beautiful children. I have neither. No kids. No husband. I have been in a relationship with a woman for almost seven years, it has not been easy, but I am living for me.

I do not like limits or being confined to ANYTHING. Hell, even my phone plan must be unlimited in every aspect. I do not like limits. Which is hilarious considering the length of my current relationship.

When I was pregnant, my biggest fear was that I'd lose myself. I didn't want to ONLY be a mother. This seems shallow and some of you may frown upon these words, but I have witnessed a cycle and it never fails. Woman meets man, gets pregnant, cares for child, works, pays bills, cares for man, barely rests, and has meltdowns occasionally. All the while, who cares for her? I have asked, "What about you?" to so many women that I've crossed paths with. I received no answers. I can't lie, this scared the hell out of me. I love the idea of having a family, but this reality made me want to seriously run for my life.

Many of you are overwhelmed, overworked, and overfucked. You are unappreciated and possibly hiding in closets to cry sporadically; you are tired. You have little to no support and the world is constantly caving in on you. This is what kept me far away from the American Dream, but very close to the judgement of others. Judgment. I thought that we as American people were done being so damn judgmental. I guess that went out of the window with world peace. I have dived into quite a bit, but I am merely getting started. Insecurity also lies in the perception of others.

To be pretty in this world means to equate to a model, be lusted after, and possess a flat stomach with a fat behind. So many women have morphed into this stereotypical image. To keep myself from feeling unworthy or unattractive, I aimed to acquire those qualities. As women, we want to feel beautiful, sexy even, so we do what it takes in order to make ourselves feel that way. For me, that began with the phases I discussed earlier in this chapter, but when I became an adult, I had to step my cookies up. I noticed women getting butt lifts, breast implants, and weight loss procedures. I attempted to lose weight the old fashion way repeatedly, it worked until it didn't.

I then began to fancy myself with the stress of finding the perfect makeup. I started with a Bare Minerals powder in 2013 and then transitioned to a MAC foundation around late 2015. I only wore foundation because I was a novice when it came to other areas of makeup.

My longing for acceptance in the world of beauty did not prevent the catty comments, the rolling of eyes, or the awkward moments in my relationship. There were times when girls made my partner feel as though she were dating two different people. For example, if she got into an altercation with a friend, they'd tear me down to disturb her, *"She's only cute because she wears all that makeup."* I was scrutinized for wanting to be pretty, all compliments of something that merely enhanced my skin and elevated my confidence. Why did they care so much? Nobody will ever

I am Porcelain

make me resort back to an image that I wanted to change. I didn't know what to think or how to feel. My partner eventually did begin to feel like I was two different people, *maybe I was*.

With makeup, I was sassy, mouthy, confident, happy, and ready to take on the world. Without it, I was moody, not ready for the day, didn't want to be bothered, and I was not upbeat. The same pattern followed with my hair, clothes, nails, and toes. It's almost as if these things MADE me. I spent so much time wondering what the answer was when I knew it all along. These things in fact, DID make me. This is where we have fallen as women. I used to sulk in what people have said about me and it would make me feel so awful, but I will not spend another moment defending my face, hair, body or lifestyle to anyone. Not anymore.

I decided to try something with myself and it began with not blocking others from my life but blocking me from theirs. I deactivated my Facebook and I created a vision tailored to me. I want to be happy with who I see staring back at me in the mirror when the wigs are gone, when the makeup is gone, and when the clothes come off. I want to be happy with me.

I am Porcelain

Social media is exhausting and depressing. I constantly compared myself to so many people in my newsfeed; I wanted to do what they were doing, look like them, be happy like them. Is it possible? I wondered. Was it all simply a hoax? I could not tell. I just knew that so many people had the life that I wanted, and I was just living through them with a pain in my heart. Something had to give. Little did I know, it'd be me.

The flaw in a lot of us is that we aim to destroy people who commit to changing, all because we know who they used to be. I'm sure that you've encountered the never-ending story of the girl/guy that left town to pursue a dream, right? They worked hard and when they finally succeeded, they continued to thrive, far away from a home that was no longer a home to them anymore. In situations such as this, this person is labeled as a sellout and is constantly reminded of who they were; Negative Nancie's want to pin you to your past. Don't let them. We only want to run from the worst versions of ourselves.

For some, "home" is what raped their sisters in the next room, "home" is where their mother was beaten, where THEY were beaten or molested. "Home" is where their loved ones were murdered. Home. Home was never a home,

I am Porcelain

only a house of pain with windowpanes that painted growing pains.

So, stop trying to tether people to what is bound to ruin them, even if it is as simple as their outer beauty. Never allow anyone to annihilate your identity.

You determine who you wish to become and how you want to look. *When you conform to the thoughts of others, you allow pieces of yourself to die on the inside.*

I am Porcelain; The Naked Truth

P is for Power.

I am Porcelain

Forgive me Father, for I have sinned

I said that I'd tell you my lies and my deepest darkest secrets, didn't I? Well, I've been a bad bad girl, if I do say so myself. I mentioned that I dated quite a bit. Some of my experiences were great and others, not so much. There was a boy- ha, don't the best stories begin that way? Any who, there was boy. His name, I shall not speak of. I knew him from Jr. high and was terrified of him, he was not at all my type. However, we fell in love. I saw a very nice side of him during one of my last summers in high school. Our relationship didn't last very long because he left for military training and soon after, we cheated on one another. We were young, so no hard feelings were there, we moved on.

Eventually, we got back together, and I was faithful, we were even talking marriage. I was sending letters, lots of letters, and I was happy. I found out that he was cheating on me; he was apparently in a relationship when we proclaimed our love for one another. He was unaware that I knew. I found out who the girl was, and I began to plot from that day

I am Porcelain

forward. I played nice with him although I was very upset; I needed to consort with the crazy women in my head to see how *"we"* wanted to punish him. I was going to ruin his relationship; he was in love with her. He had the nerve to tell me that he wanted the both of us, and that he wanted me to be ONE of his baby's mothers. Who the hell had I become? Who did he think that I was? He was bat-shit crazy. I set out to let him know that I was too.

I found out that his Perfect Patty used to attend the same high school as I, so it was game on. I dated him because he wasn't my type, I thought that he was safe. Silly me. I had him come to visit me when he came into town. I heard that he had been screwing his beloved in a car, I made sure that he rented a hotel before he came to pick me up, because if he planned on "tapping" this, it would be at a cost. He didn't know that he would be paying for more than what he purchased. Let the festivities begin.

I was getting my intel from someone that was close to her. They told me everything. I felt bad for what I was about to do because she was a really nice girl, but he was a piece of shit, I considered my antics to be a favor to us all.

We made it to the room and had sex multiple times, unprotected. I could have simply lied about having sex with

I am Porcelain

him and passed it along, so that it could get to her but no, I wanted it to be true. I had to get him back... I wasn't done. I strung him along after this and told my mutual party that linked me to her.

I also told "our" boyfriend sometime after that I was pregnant before fading into the wind of a new relationship. This got back to her and they were finished, mission accomplished. But I was still not done. *"Finish him Britt"* was all I heard. One night while lying in bed with my new boyfriend, I texted what would soon be my ex to let him know that I miscarried. He was crushed. I let him go and moved on with my life, never revealing my lie. To this day, he is convinced that I lost a baby of his. I didn't feel bad until I saw that he was actually sad about it. Eventually he and I were okay again, as friends. I thought to tell him that it was lie, but I charged it to the game as my revenge on him. I also thought to confess so that I could hurt him even more, but- let's not cry over spilled milk, right? I was feeling great and had moved on a couple times after him by then.

I am 28 years old now and reflecting back on this truly puts my stomach in knots because around 2 years later, I endured the worst miscarriage ever, and it was very much real. Talk about irony. I was very vindictive, I should clear

I am Porcelain

the air and relinquish this truth to him, maybe I will after all. Life has a way of catching up with us. It caught up with him too but we're talking about me right now, so- NEXT.

What else have I done? Hmm well for another start, I could relay that the inconsistencies in my relationships are mostly because I have sex and ask questions later. Nothing wrong with sex, right? Well it is if it isn't with whom you're dating. Because I had been sexually active at an early age, intercourse was the answer to everything for me. I cheated a lot when I was young, and I never realized how badly I was hurting who I was with. I know that I am not alone in this analysis. I mean, are we clearly just fucked up people or are we suffering somewhere too? I didn't really care back then, but now I'm like *girl, your body count is questionable. What's wrong with you?*

I'd be lying if I said that it wasn't fun. I have mad stories to tell when I am old and grey. I was busted by the cops for having sex in a car before, like super busted. Like, pants barely covering my ass and vagina busted. I cannot –. I was also "getting the treatment" on high school grounds once upon time. My cherry was popped with some fingers. What does that even mean? I was just all over the place. No literally, ALL over the place. I have had sex at and in some wild places, but we will save those for another book.

I mentioned that I have been in a same sex relationship for 7 years now. My goodness how time flies. It was only yesterday that I sat in my car and cried to GOD because his child was falling for a girl. I remember the tears. I wonder what he thinks of me now. I felt that in the first stages of our relationship, I had no protection. I wasn't used to the judgment. Being gay was worse than being black in a predominantly white neighborhood. Yes, I said that. Read it again.

I battled my sexuality as a sophomore in high school. I was forewarned before entering the grounds of Eastern Hills High School. I was told *"they are going to get you."* I laughed everyone off and told them *"not me."* There is that irony laughing at me again. I was so tempted to be with girls. I flirted, kissed, and led them all on. I didn't engage in the "real" sexual parts of it though. I fought very hard to avoid the very many impulses in taking that next step because I knew that it would change my life. This lasted for a while until I became serious with a girl that I was friends with. After we became more than friends, still nothing sexual, we were however emotionally bound to one another, I quickly threw my towel in and ran back to what was normal for me, boys. I don't think she was surprised, she understood. I was so upset with myself because I went against my religion and I just knew in my heart that I was disappointing God, so that was enough for me to never look back.

Years passed by, but I still found myself toying with girls and women, I was "taken" by some of them. I found myself more drawn to women, even while almost marrying the last man that I was ever with. I crept closer and closer to the edge of having sex with a woman. I allowed one of my more experienced friends the pleasure of utilizing her fingers on me one drunken night after leaving a club. I liked it but she was already with someone, so I steered clear of her. Not too long after, my partner sent me a message on Facebook. I looked into her profile and after seeing how cute she was, I made up in my mind that I had to have her. She and I conversed for a bit, little flirting here and there- we exchanged numbers; I ended up head over heels for her. I could write an entire book about our sexual encounters alone. I was introduced to an entirely new world. The crazy thing is that while writing the first version of this book, I completed this section by stating that I had conquered my battle with my sexuality. I thought that it'd only be fair to fill

I am Porcelain

you all in on the truth. It is so hard to run from what pulls you harder than gravity.

I tried to keep this relationship a secret at first, but I failed, poorly. I am such a transparent person that my family was bound to find out. I wasn't aware of what I had gotten myself into. We were subjected to so much turmoil together, I feel that I threw myself to the wolves. She was used to it but eventually I had to stop and ask her, *"is this really what it's like?"*

I experienced moments where I was told that I didn't deserve help because of my "lifestyle" and co-workers verbally dragged me until it became unbearable. Something wanted me to end my life, I could feel it, but I am much stronger than that. I had never felt like such an outcast in my entire life. I still do. But it is a battle that I chose, so here I stand, still fighting. It was one thing to deal with hatred, blank stares, and shit-talking from strangers, but to deal with it from family was beneath me; I had never judged any of them. I was hurt beyond my core. I always asked myself, "What are they saying now?" and "Will they accept her, us, now?"

I thought that I could successfully navigate through life and just distance myself from certain temptations, but

I am Porcelain

this was one that met my face too many times. I recall crying every day and night for the first few months and then in spirts after that. Who was I kidding? I wasn't ready for this.

I needed to make sense of this world, but I could not. I worked at a company that is well known, so I didn't expect their employees to blatantly disrespect me when they found out that I dated a woman. There are so many statements that stain my brain while being on their clock. -

"Don't you want kids?"

"Don't you want to get married one day?"

"You know it's wrong, right?"　　　　-Male Idiot

"You serve the wrong GOD because you think it's okay to be gay."

"You need a big dick. The biggest dick."

"If you weren't eating that stuff, you wouldn't be coughing up that cold."

"You're going to hell."　　– The Classic Christian Woman.

What did I say? What did I do? I tried to be humble. It takes a lot for me to get out of character because when I go there, I GO THERE. I was afraid for anyone to see me that way. I felt bullied, and I felt so small, but who was I to take on the world? Everybody had something to say, I did not understand. I was hoping that GOD was still on my side and that he knew that I was still good, worthy of his love. But was I? I didn't know.

    I still smiled throughout my work shifts and built bonds with those of whom loved me regardless of my sexuality. Love kills pain on the bad days sometimes. When my mechanisms didn't work, I'd get upset but then I'd be forced to remember that I was on the clock and that I shouldn't act out, I should remain professional. I was eaten away by guilt and disappointment. This world was new, and it hurt. If you are contemplating being with someone of the same sex, I won't steer you from it, but I will say that you must have tough skin to live this lifestyle. The entitlement of evil thoughts, actions, and treatment emerge, and you have no choice but to accept it because it is a major part of the package that you signed up for. I was an iceberg standing firmly in front of a furnace; big, tall, and frozen on the inside. It'd take a while to diminish my presence but in due time, it would happen. I honestly wouldn't have wished this pain on anyone, and I've wished some pretty horrible things. Was it all karma or some sick and twisted way for me to realize that I would not win this battle because the battle was beyond me? I still did not know. I ignored as much as I could, but I had my limits, as anyone would.

The employees of this company also slandered me in front of customers. I was speechless for months. Bullying was in the chapter of Elementary, I didn't think that I'd have to revisit it again. I usually stood up for myself, but I couldn't with this. Eventually one day on my shift, this same Christian woman approached me. She and I had some words regarding a break that I had taken prior to her approach. She wanted to make it her duty to let me know that because I am a homosexual, it's out of line for me to tell her to kiss my ass. So, it wasn't inappropriate because she was my elder but because I am gay? Oh okay. We had a problem now. I politely informed her that within the duration of my employment, nearly every word she has spoken to me had been "out of line."

After that moment, I reported her, and it became a major deal within the company, not because they don't tolerate harassment or discrimination against religion or sexuality, but because they didn't want to give me justice. Management even advised me not to tell anyone about what was going on. They were not going to fuck me, and then tell me to be quiet about it, I had to let them know that I make

I am Porcelain

noises when I fuck; I set forth to find my own justice. This job was both the best and worst thing that ever happened to me. I loved my friends, but those days and nights crying in their bathrooms because of everything that I had been subjected to, was not fair to me. I fought hard to get justice within the company but because of that, they fired me; retaliation. I went into a major depression for a couple of years and didn't want to work, due to the fear of being treated this way again. Eventually, I did obtain a new job. I developed a horrible anxiety because I didn't want anyone to know that I was with a woman. I felt crazy and alone. I drank. A lot. Between losing my mother, my sanity, and my job, I was spiraling. I took it all out on my partner. She was there for it all, but I couldn't shake bearing the pain. I turned up a bottle every night and became bitter and angry. My drinking put me in dangerous situations. I was so aggressive and daring that I jumped out of a moving car onto a dark road in Everman, Texas one night. Luckily the car wasn't going too fast, but I was pretty banged up. Thighs were bruised up, I couldn't stand the next day, and not to mention, my wig came off because my partner tried to grab me before I threw my big ass out onto the curb. My wig wasn't secure, and neither was I.

I am Porcelain

My partner attempted to stop me from drinking so much, it didn't work for a while but then one day, I decided that the cycle of alcoholism in my family had to stop. I was so belligerent, ignorant, and abusive. My partner was the nicest person that I had ever met, so how could I have treated her this way? I was out of control. I felt justified in my behaviors because I am a firm believer in speaking and doing what I feel, but I must say that this is a twisted way of thinking. I still struggle with being rational and understanding that I cannot do what I think or feel, not because I literally cannot, but because there are consequences for all actions, even mine.

The bruises that I woke up to on my legs told me something. They said "Bitch- you are tripping"- I was not convinced. I went to the hospital at some point due to an infection because I was only drinking beer, vodka, tequila, Cîroc, and wine. I woke up early in the morning grabbing beers. I was fine, leave it to me. My father advised me to stop drinking as well, I didn't listen to him. I eventually stopped after a couple of years. I thank GOD for allowing me to stop on my own. I began getting sick after I'd drink, so it forced me to stop. The same thing happened to my mother, but it took extreme measures for her recovery. I get my stubbornness from her and my grandmother, *it's hard to fight*

I am Porcelain

past what feels natural. I have matured a lot, and I am able to continue to grow, reflecting on my past and realizing that I cannot revert back to those ways. It may seem like nothing to somebody, but my anger had become so uncontrollable that sometimes I'd pass out and the paramedics would have to be called. There'd be a showering shimmer of lights before I'd hit the floor. The anger from my experiences had taken over me.

I sit in awe sometimes, and I see the younger version of myself fighting a world that was much bigger than her. I was forewarned by many people to stop pursuing a case against the company that I worked for. They told me that I'd lose my job and that it wasn't worth it; I didn't care about losing my job because I had already lost myself. Management told me that if I hadn't cursed at this woman when she bothered me about my break, then maybe they would've been able to something about it.

I told myself that a promiscuous woman can still cry rape; My case should've been treated the same. Even if I cursed, I broke a company rule, she broke something much bigger.

I see that girl now, myself that day. She left the office in a rage, face flooded with tears and choking on the word, "why?". Her false eyelashes had come off and her makeup had run down her face, uncovering that little girl that she had been hiding the entire time. She was disappointed.

The woman who haunted me throughout my employment attended my mother's funeral. This proclaimed woman of GOD knew the type of human that I was and yet, she still reminded me of a sin that I was already at war with. She was nice to me sometimes, which was fine, but she gave into her own flesh just to let me know how disgusting she thought I was.

I wish that my mother could have risen from her casket to put this woman out, that would've been nice. I did what I could though, and that's what we must remember when we face the battles that we are up against every day. Never give up on yourselves; *we have survivors and activists in our bloodlines.* I hope that you know that, and I hope that you take this message for what it is. I have buried this story into this book for you and your growth. We can't win all the time.

I do wish that I could see that version of myself again because I would hug her and tell her that she did well. The Store Manager had no regard for what he and his employees had done to me, which left me with no regrets for how I handled the situation. I was given bible pamphlets directed to scriptures about me being an abomination, I was forced to feel as though I should have killed myself, -thinking maybe then, they'd hear me. *This was wrong and I just knew it in my soul.* I haven't been able to go into this store without my throat closing up and feeling overheated, so, I don't go. I can't go. I won't go. I separated myself from everyone, friends included, I was more than overwhelmed. I wasn't here. Regardless of what they used to defeat me; I know that this was not okay. I have faith that even now, justice will be served. May GOD grant you justice in your battles as well.

This experience was a very touchy subject for me and though, I didn't share every single detail, I feel naked. As if you can see me, as if you can see her.

You see, during that time, Gay Marriage was being celebrated, so it only made the light that shined so brightly on me- burn, stinging my skin from the attention and melting the porcelain in which I had been molded into. I then remembered my grandmother saying *"Brittiny, you know them thangs break,"* because I had been broken.

Every clump of clay used to create that ashtray reminded me of what I had become to this world; something that it could smash its lit sticks inside of, leaving its remains,

I am Porcelain

as I withered away, *breaking off, chipping apart* until there was no more of me.

I am Porcelain

I am Porcelain; The Naked Truth

Can't quite let go.

I am Porcelain

Invested Afflictions

  I poured my heart into this book because the pain that I've held onto for so long, had to go somewhere. Death introduced itself to me at a very young age; I didn't understand it or why it had to happen. I witnessed others lose their loved ones and I hated it; it was hard to watch. I was okay until I began to lose people closer and closer into my circle. It felt like my heart was caving in and I would never be allowed to breathe again. I began to become so nervous about death and its randomness that I feared for the nonexistence of my own life. That's where poetry began for me.

  Realize that I am human and that I am relinquishing my truths to you so that you may see that you are not alone; *WE* are not alone. We just think that we are because a lot of times when we suffer, we run and hide to hurt alone, only to end up suffering from depression or becoming even more distraught. We disappear when we should be connecting with people who have or are enduring the same pain. We fail to realize that there are people that will cry with us and hold US while WE cry. There are people that will stand with us as if they were there from the beginning; there are people that care. I am one of those people.

Although portions of my past are embarrassing, I am open about it now because maybe and hopefully my mistakes will warn somebody, save somebody. Anybody. When I lost my virginity at the tender age of 12, I was forced to grow up due to the interest that I carried in older men. The way that I had begun to carry myself came natural to me; I was a very serious child. I wanted more attention than what my family could give to me. There were several other children and they were younger than I. Therefore, I took it upon myself to fill that void. There I was, impulsively diving into journeys that I was not quite ready for, again. Sex was my answer for every ounce of frustration, and misunderstanding, but most of all, it was my answer for pain.

My grandmother stayed buried in cooking, cleaning, and preparing us for school every day. By the time she finished, she grew tired as anyone would. I know that she and my mother were always there but something in me yearned for more.

Truth be told, I wish that someone would've kept me tucked away from this world. Truth be told, I was searching for all of the wrong things. Truth, I'm not even sure that I cared.

I am Porcelain

I subconsciously felt that I was obligated to have my own "somebody," or as many "somebodies" as I saw fit. It never registered to me how dangerous this was, and even once I found out, I disregarded the signs because sex did something for me. It was an adventure that I continuously wanted to explore. To have someone in my reach whenever I needed or wanted them to be, felt right to me. I was convinced.

I faced my first scare of an STD at the age of 14. I was given Chlamydia. I had never saw my grandmother more disappointed than when I handed her a piece of paper in which reflected the list of my sexual partners. My recollection is 5 when it should have been 0. I was scared for a long time to do anything but similar to an addict, I got that itch again.

Fast forwarding to 2009, I was dating left and right. I rode this wave relentlessly until guys began to bore me. I strolled right into danger zone when this man caught me coming out of a clothing store with my brother. He fit my type, which was bright skinned with long hair, and he was charming, so I took his number. I texted him eventually and we immediately became exclusive. This relationship was tragically short. There was a major age gap, he was 28, which was fine with me; I was 18. He and I grew close, I

I am Porcelain

even grew fond of his daughter. Her mother didn't like that very much, she showed that by bashing out the window on my mother's SUV. I couldn't even begin to explain it to her when I returned with her car, luckily, she wasn't upset. She understood the lengths of a jealous woman.

    I practically lived there, but I left every so often. My grandmother resided in walking distance, which was convenient, but I was definitely not walking to any man. Any who, he found out that his mother was diagnosed with breast cancer, which broke him. I'm sure that it would've broken any man. His mother owned the clothing store where we met, it was their family business.

    I knew that he was not in a good space because he had begun to act differently towards me; he changed. I say this because he began to drink heavily, aimlessly pushing me away. I became confused as to where we stood, so I came over less, I should've never gone back. I couldn't reach him one night, so I did what we crazy women refer to as a "pop up"- in which is where we stop by one's home or location, unannounced. SURPRISE, Right? No, the surprise was on me. I took my mother's car and set forth. My ears tuned in on the loud music as I approached his door, my worry transitioned to anger as I knocked. He opened the door, eyes glazed and body still, he was startled. A drunk is all that I could see before me. He stood back and allowed me to enter, not saying a word. I did a sweep of the room. I was able to see one slut and a group of his friends. I was so pissed off that I eventually left and went back home. He apologetically reached out to me.

I returned the next night or so; I usually drove there but this particular time, my mother transported me. As soon as I stepped in, I witnessed the same shenanigans; people hanging out in his living room, drinking. My blood was boiling because he asked me to come over for just US to spend time together; I realize now that it was just his stiff dick doing the talking. To avoid confrontation, I just went straight to his room and eventually went to bed. A few hours passed, I was woken up by his heavy stomach lying on my back and drunk wet kisses; they sent unwanted chills down my spine. I wasn't fully awake, but I squirmed and showed rejection to his foreplay so that I could return to my dreams. I turned my head over to the right side of the bed and glanced at the clock that set below the tv; it read between 3:00 am and 4:00 am. I turned back to face the wall again. He began to grind on the backside of my body, I still would not give in. I was still livid with him. I only wanted to sleep at this point. My eyes were still closed, I felt myself getting more upset, so I began to curse at him. I recall saying "Hell no"

I am Porcelain

and "Get the fuck off of me!" He must've mistaken my anger and choice of words for "Come and get it" because he utilized his forearm to pin me down, as he undid his pants and snatched my panties below my cheeks. I was a worm, wiggling to greet the surface but instead, I was face down in his pillow, going nowhere.

  In the midst of disregarding my tears and cries to be released, he took his tool and shoved it inside of my ass with no remorse. As I moved my head from side to side, he bent down and whispered into my right ear his version of encouraging words, which were "Calm down" and "Relax." He then added "Just for a little while," as if I were given a damn choice. I can't help but to picture the sheets in which I gripped, pillowcases in which I shed tears on, and the wall that remained one of my only witnesses. By then of course, he didn't plan to exit until he finished what he started. I continued to move, to cry, but he continued to rape me. I heard a loud pop come from my anal area, indicating that something had gone wrong. My eyes grew big. *What had he done to me?* I didn't know, but it hurt like hell. Involuntary sex is more excruciating than anything that I could ever imagine. I felt like a straight man in prison waiting for a righteous guard to save me, only no one came, but him. I clenched my fingers and used my fists to beat the pillows.

I am Porcelain

Eventually I laid there, numb, paralyzed. I wished that I could use my feet to kick my own ass for believing that he only wanted my presence in the first place. None of my efforts succeeded.

When he finished, I jumped up and ran into the bathroom- instead of running home like I should have. I remember using damn near the entire roll of toilet paper to wipe away the blood and semen, but I had absolutely nothing to wipe away the pain. It ached my rear to stand or sit, but I had to do one or the other. I walked over to the sink to clean myself up and as I stared into the mirror, my crying became a low sob. The woman that stared back at me was more than I could ever be, because although I saw tears and a girl that needed somebody, she saw strength in me.

I washed up and used my legs to carry me where my heart could not. I was more than fragile. *I was shattered.* I could barely walk and what's worse than that is I don't even remember if he was there when I returned or not. I laid there motionless, in shock, trying to make sense of what had just happened. The words "You hurt me" managed to slip from my lips, but silence was the only thing that responded to me.

One night and a system full of drinks gave him the gall to rape me. He and I were supposed to be… something, but that didn't stop him from destroying me in my prime of

I am Porcelain

becoming a woman. As time moved forward, I realized that I possessed more than tears from this experience; there was anger, fear, and disbelief. I couldn't accept that he gave absolutely zero fucks for what he had done to me. I made excuses for his actions and battled with so many voices in my head, attempting to escape the truth of it all; denial. I was so obsessed with focusing on the good in everyone that I truly gathered that he was empathetic and sorry, when in actuality, he was neither.

Typically, when women are raped, we presume this involves a penis entering the vaginal area without consent. Anal sex was deeply desired in this case, so, for me, it was much worst. The alcohol that crawled against my face when he whispered "Just relax"- didn't make the shit any better; nor did the rolling of tears, the kicking of my feet, the screaming of my lungs, or the aching or my soul. I was hoping that someone heard me because I didn't want to be the girl who was raped but was too scared to utter a fucking word; yet there I was. Here I am; THAT GIRL. I harbored guilt and I felt that I was to blame because once upon a time, I condoned anal sex in our relationship. I put a stop to it because I began to feel uncomfortable with his obsession of screwing me anally. I had found a box full of sex tapes and videos while cleaning one day; this made me questioned who

I am Porcelain

I had been sleeping with. There were just so many, more than what seemed normal to me. I informed him of my desire to no longer indulge in anal sex, and he said that he was "cool" with it. I believed for years that because I allowed it, it was a result of him abusing me *the way* that he did.

I was sure that my screams carried onto the other side of the wall, regardless of how smothered they were. They were loud, clear, and heartfelt to me. His friend, in which I knew was there never moved a muscle. His friend never even tried to save me. I wondered what type of man could do something like that. I wondered if he would hear MY cries in HIS sleep at some point, or if one day, HE would smother in MY tears. I will never know.

My rapist was never punished for what happened, not on my account. The first time that I saw him after all of this, I was exiting a beauty supply store. Right there on the sidewalk stood him and his new woman. I was alone. Suddenly he and I were in the *Twilight Zone*, where I was a ghost from his past. The second he saw me, he froze. I anxiously moved forward with no words. He raped me in the year of 2010, I swept it under a rug, but seeing him one year later, brought back every skeleton that I thought I had tucked away forever. I just couldn't believe it. I really could not believe it. Here it was, I murdered him in my mind time and

I am Porcelain

time again but there he was, very much alive and breathing… IN MY FACE.

After that moment, I began to have nightmares. There were times when I wasn't sleep but somehow, I'd space out for moments, visualizing what he had done to me; the only thing that I could picture was that night. I would see the same scene over and over again, no matter where I would be or how badly I would aim to *"think happy thoughts."* I could literally smell that same alcohol on his breath from that same night. I also dreamt that those around me were raping me too; friends, strangers, my current boyfriend, hell- the damn garbage man.

The rape of Brittiny Deshon Morehead seared into my brain and forced me to watch myself get raped at parties, apartment complexes by the dumpster, and back to where it all began, in the bedroom of someone who was supposed to be my boyfriend.

Prior to this experience, I associated rape with strangers; and then I learned that rape can be as close as home. I wish forgetting were just as easy as breathing, but sometimes taking a breath is the hardest thing to do, when you feel like you're dying. My soul was so lost. I don't believe that it's lost now, I just know that it's somewhere it shouldn't be. Unfortunately, I don't believe in ruining

I am Porcelain

someone's life over a mistake. Bear with me. I use the word *mistake* as a blanket for myself. I don't want to know that I dated a rapist; I'm not even sure if that's just who he *was* or is. However, I know that he will have to answer to GOD. I honestly just needed an apology worth believing, but I never did receive it.

After he raped me, he sent me text messages trying to get me to come back over. He claimed to have *missed me so much.* I rejected him along with explaining why I refused to come. His reply to me was "I don't remember, but can you please come over?" My body must've gone into shock because I couldn't- not even for one second believe what he had texted me. I was stunned and livid, unsure on how to handle my response.

He didn't remember, but I remembered perfectly. The blood that made its way into the toilet every time that I visited the bathroom, remembered perfectly. I recall staring at it just hoping that the existence of that night would follow the tissue and the waste, but it never did. Now again, he and I were texting, so imagine my surprise to not even a phone call after I told him that he raped me. How inconsiderate was he? I knew this had to be his stiff dick again, or could it be that he was revealing himself to me all along? From that day

I am Porcelain

forward, I never backtracked. I kept my distance. He never even asked me for forgiveness.

Memories are more taunting than nightmares because not only are they real, they hardly ever go away. When I did decide to move on, I moved on with my best friend after telling him what this jackass had done to me. He and I had a very quick and unfortunate ending as well. We were even supposed to get married. After 5 years of friendship, you'd think we were the perfect fit, but I grew tired of his malicious ways. We should have remained friends.

Toward the ending of our relationship, I reconnected with a friend that I used to work with, a male. While confiding in him, we fell in love. We even ended up living together. I had to expose the secret of being raped to him because when I'd have a bowel movement, he'd literally have to come and help me. *Why didn't I just go to the Doctor already?* It's simple, I was afraid to. The stretching of my anal area hurt in an unusual way when I'd have to rid my body of its waste. It makes my skin crawl and my soul cries every time I think about it. I look back as the woman that I have become now, and I feel so stupid. I must really say that standing in front of a mirror and undressing all of my secrets is the hardest thing to do, but I feel that it's necessary.

iBleedPoetry

I am Porcelain

I was taken advantage of sexually before, but there are just some hardships a girl can't cover up so easily. I can't just brush them all away and expect the wind to carry my skeletons elsewhere, because at some point, the bones always find their way back to me.

I was ruthless with my sexual activity; maybe even the fact that I didn't mind dating older men was due to my being a Fatherless Child, but I hate clichés, so I never accepted this as a possibility. I do know that if he was present back then, things would have gone much differently for me. The crazy thing is that my father returned into my life the year that I was raped. I feared losing him; it's as though GOD sent him to me because just with my tone during one phone call, he knew what happened to me. He knew that I needed him, and he never left me again.

I don't want another little girl to waste her life growing up the way that I did because she'll turn out to be me or much worse. Any form of writing always helped me cope with what I was dealing with but poetry, *poetry spoke life into me the way that Jesus did Lazarus (John 11).*

I put my life, love, and heart into the wrong hands while growing up. I am just so thankful that GOD put a halt in my journey, before it was too late. I thought that I was done with pain when I found out that I'd be having my own

I am Porcelain

bundle of joy in the year of 2012. Two of my sisters already had children of their own; I just knew that it was my time too. The uncertainty in my stomach told me otherwise. I would've much rather been beaten to death than to have lost what quickly changed my life. I thought that I would quickly get over this, I was wrong.

It was March 3, 2012. I had spent the day with my father's side of the family. While I was out with them, my little brother pointed at my stomach in the back of my dad's car and told me, "There's a baby in there." He had the biggest grin on his face and all I could think was "What the fuck!" I was picking up weight, but I didn't look pregnant, and although I was already having thoughts of a possible pregnancy, I was almost certain that I was not. *I never get pregnant* is what I kept telling myself. I shrugged his comment off by saying *"nope, just fat."* My Mama Vern *(my father's mother, my grandmother)* asked me if there was any truth to what my brother was saying, I laughed at her, responding "no maim."

I texted my boyfriend to laugh at what had just happened; I arrived home to three pregnancy tests. It was normal for me to have irregular cycles but this particular time, I missed a cycle, so we were both naturally curious. All

I am Porcelain

three tests read PREGNANT. Our eyes grew wide with shock and happiness. We were so happy.

He rushed me to a hospital; they tested my blood and urine and then told us that I was "very pregnant." We laughed at the nurse and simply gazed at one another in shock. We didn't make it home until 5 am. I called my inner circle to share the news; I was 4 weeks pregnant. My twin sister and my best friend were happier than I was. I could hear my grandmother's smile through the phone and my mother, well, she was Kim. She asked me *"Brittiny, what you gone do with a baby?"* her response upset me, but she and I were one in the same. We wouldn't necessarily *choose* to have children. *I wish she were here to upset me again.*

It was honestly a wonderful moment. The joy that came over us was more than I had experienced before. I had already began wanting to shop for our baby, pick out names, get custom jewelry- the whole 9. I even wanted to open a savings account for him/her. I was in and out of the hospital every weekend. They insisted that we were great, but I just knew that we weren't. I was so paranoid and after experiencing what happened next, I see that I had every right to be. I made my last visit to O B Triage and it was time for me to get my first sonogram, we were so excited. I was changed into a hospital gown and my feet were placed into

I am Porcelain

the stirrups; the Doctor began. There was an uncomfortable silence that filled the room, I almost prepared myself for bad news because this was just too good to be true. The preparation failed because the moment that the Doctor relayed to us that my pregnancy was abnormal, my heart sank lower than an anchor. He explained to me that since I was over my second month, we should have heard a heartbeat, but we didn't because he or she didn't have a heart.

    I broke down screaming. I was in their emergency room last week, due to pain and an odd color of blood in my underwear. I was told that these things were no issue because it meant that my uterus was expanding, so bleeding and pain was to be expected. From this visit, I took the pain with a smile and no meds because I was happy to be in pain for him/her; I was under the impression that our baby was just growing. Little did I know, he/she was running away from me.

    After replaying all of this in my head, the Doctor in Triage told me that our baby stopped growing at week 5, so for 4 weeks, all of the pain that I felt was our baby aborting itself. Now after hearing the worst thing that I had ever heard (and I've heard some pretty bad shit), they informed me that I must return for a procedure where they will scrape the

I am Porcelain

remains of our baby, out of me (DNC). Everything in my body shattered because the mother that I was becoming, did not want to give up the only existence of her seed. All I had so far were pregnancy tests and Baby Elmo books. I refused. They forewarned me that the further I held off, the sicker I would become. I left the hospital devastated and worn out from crying so hard. Something in my mind told me to stand firm on my decision to keep the remains of my baby inside me. The damage had been done, until I made it to my grandmother's house the following day. My family was aware of our loss. They were also aware of what was being required of me. My mother and grandmother tried to convince me to do the DNC and they assured me that I would be fine, but I didn't want to be; I was supposed to be a mother. I fell to my knees, my mother held me, and I recall uttering the words "I was supposed to have a baby." Chills ran through my body and I began to throw up. My granny couldn't bear to watch me in this state, she walked away with her head down. My grandmother always had a really soft spot for me, she hurts when I hurt. This hurt me even more because I wanted my grandmother to bond with my child the way she had with me. My mom continued to rub my back and console me. This was just the beginning of my melt downs. My mom and boyfriend rubbed my back as I laid

I am Porcelain

across my grandmother's floor like a wounded animal. Eventually after managing to stand, I went home.

My boyfriend proposed to me the night that we found out about our loss. I said yes, and although I was happy, I couldn't find it in my heart to enjoy the engagement because I was processing the news of no longer being a mother. I respected him, a lot. For him to have gotten down on his knee in our bedroom, to proclaim his love to me, whether I was with child or not, proved to me that he loved me; *baby or not, I was who he wanted to marry.*

Days went on and my display of pain became more frequent. Because of this, my boyfriend spent several nights peeling me from the floor and talking me to sleep; I took my miscarriage very hard. The kitchen happened to be a place that caused me to have suicidal thoughts, probably because the knives were summoning my flesh. I never knew. They tried to make love to my skin, I almost gave in. I had been in situations before where I wanted to harm myself but this time, it went beyond a rush; I wanted to die. Every time I drove somewhere, I'd imagine myself running the car over the bridge or into another car. I wanted to see what would happen to me, however, due to my fear of no longer being here, I couldn't do it. I imagined how my loved ones would feel if I had done something like that, the possibility of their pain broke my heart.

I ended up getting the DNC after my mother told me that holding onto the remains of a fetus could be fatal. They had to sedate me for this procedure. While the nurses prepped me, I was given a dose of the sedative through an IV in a vein on my hand. Yes, my hand. I was in excruciating pain. I recall my fiancé sitting next to me and telling me that he wished it were him and not me. He made me feel so loved and so appreciated for enduring what life was putting me through. My damaged ass pushed him away because that's what I do. I push people away.

I couldn't successfully create a new chapter with him because I was emotionally invested in pieces of the last one. I refused to try to get pregnant again. The first time wasn't even planned, I surely didn't want to suffer mentally with the possible fail of another. I didn't want to replace what we lost and the fact that people felt that we should try again, offended me.

Along the way, I recognized that I should have said no to his proposal because I completely shut down from him. I wouldn't let him touch me and if he did, I would snap shortly into what was supposed to be intercourse. It was a wonder he didn't cheat on me. He wasn't the type to, but I

I am Porcelain

would've if I were him. I did all that I could to stay out of the house; I worked on my writing more, visited my family, ran errands, -anything that kept me alone. I stopped having sex with for a while. *"Get that thing away from me"* is all my mind could think when he'd try to pursue me. I distanced myself in so many ways that it began to hurt us both. I couldn't take it any longer, so I wanted out of the relationship. I was unbearable to live with. I was so angry and rebellious with him, GOD, pregnant women, women with children, and myself. I compared myself to so many people, wondering why it had to be me. I recall saying the meanest things, I blamed him for the loss of our child. I told him that maybe I'd have a child to call my own if he *were* a piece of shit like the rest of em. I didn't mean for it to be bad when I said it, but it hurt him like hell.

    I blamed myself too and even questioned the Doctor, due to my sexual history. I was exposed to Chlamydia again prior to entering this relationship, I didn't know that I had it, so it caused a Pelvic Inflammatory Disease. I explained this to the Doctor, and he assured me that PID wasn't the cause of my miscarriage. I wanted it to be. I needed some sort of explanation, but he wouldn't give me one, nor would he give me my sonogram- he said that he couldn't because it would be traumatizing for me. I just wanted to have it to hold, and to love as my first everything. I wish that I weren't an emotional wreck that day but because if I were in my right mind, he would have most certainly given me my sonogram.

  I was forced to move past this experience, but it took me so long to accept this loss; it took years. I faulted myself for having moments of anger during my pregnancy. I was always a dreamer but when the reality sank in that my life would have to change, I became disappointed and frustrated that my goals had to change too. I was angry with my fiancé because men never have to really sacrifice anything when a woman is pregnant; they can still go out, pursue career interests, and drink. Women have to worry about their health, job/career, weight gain, body changes, and feeling unattractive. I didn't want to bang the gavel on his life by telling him "WE are having a baby together, therefore WE are pregnant together." I didn't think it was fair that he could do things that I couldn't. The night we found out that I was no longer having a baby, I stood in awe on the elevator reflecting on the rants of my life changing and I asked myself if it were worth the griping about. Needless to say, it was not. I'd give anything to have this moment back now.

  I still counted the months as time drew towards the arrival of what should've been my baby. November came and I was still a mess. The only thing that I gave birth to in

I am Porcelain

a matter of months, was anger. By the time December arrived, he and I were faced with good-byes. I packed my things, footing it to my car in the snow, as he laid there on our bed, numb. My heart was colder than the winter… I was gone. Soon finding myself to be subjecting another to the wrath of my pasts not too long after. Healing is important. Counseling is important. Communication is important. Without it, we are left creating turmoil in lives of those who don't even deserve it.

There are so many things that contribute to my poetry. I encountered broken hearts, STDs, and adult-like situations before I was ready, but GOD was there for me every single time; I'm thankful for his mercy. In the hopes of changing the world one portion at a time, I hand my truths to you. I was afraid to reveal these things because I feared what everyone would portray me as, but I do like to air my own dirty laundry, so it works out for us all. Also, let the record reflect- that I do not give a fuck.

My truths are corrupted and inappropriate because my life was. I don't believe in painting false images. We are tested and broken down in the same ways, we are the same. I am here to stand the tests of time with you, to hurt with you, to love with you. I chose to handle life and not allow life to handle me.

I am Porcelain

You can hide behind locked doors all day long, running away from the things and the people that hurt you, but that can in no way possible overshadow the hurt and guilt that you carry for thinking, believing, and knowing, that all the pain caused, was and is your own fault.

Reliving these experiences as I type to share it with you all, is not what I intended to do, but in order for me to help you grasp the depths behind my poetry, I must stand here completely nude, facing you with every conviction that I could possibly possess. I write to free my soul, to free myself, and to free you. *Sharing my ugliest truths is what I am entitled to do because it connects me to the eyes that lay upon these naked pages.*

I am Porcelain; The Naked

Still in hiding.

Naked

As humans, we tend to naturally gravitate towards other people, no matter where we are. Think about it. Have you ever instantly connected to a stranger while out on your own engagement? Or do you recall being introduced to someone that made an unforgettable impression on you? I ask because in my venture to obtain employment, the goal was to stay to myself and remain professional at all times. However, since I am not a prune or uptight, my personality eventually revealed itself to those around me.

While working at the company that I mentioned in the precious chapter, I had some hardships and losses, but I also had some gains. I bonded with so many people that I was able to grieve my mother with their genuine love and support. *I had friends that would literally hold my hair while I vomited in the back of the bathroom from crying so much.* They were friends then, and they are friends now; but I learned something while working there.

There was a guy, he and I were never romantically involved; we were truly just friends. In the span of our friendship, we confided in one another about a lot of things,

I am Porcelain

so we were "tight." He saw me shed a lot of tears about my mother, but I never expected to see any of his.

We have this distorted complex that tells us "Men don't cry." This one did. I recall a day during lunch, he and I were discussing the recurring shootings of black men. I didn't realize how badly the world had become until I witnessed the fear in his eyes. I had never saw him like this before. Serious. The more he expressed his concern for our generation of black men, tears began to fall. I was completely astounded, and in that instant, I thought about how afraid every black man must've been; it was heart-wrenching and twistedly poetic to me. After this day, I channeled my perception towards men differently. It was no longer men vs. women, and that women have it harder, it was simply- no one's pain is more important than the other, because we are all hurting. *Being black just makes the pain worse sometimes.*

To be a black man is hard, very hard. There are so many expectations and so much pressure. I believe that this is why a lot of black men have laxed on their responsibilities and obligations, whether it be to their wives, careers, or children; it's too hard and too much, so they say fuck it. I've saw this up close and personal, but to be a black anything is hard. A black mother, a black father, a black child, even a

I am Porcelain

black object; BLACK just doesn't "make the cut" all too often.

Due to the constant reminder from within the black community that life will always be harder because of our skin color. I created a particular mind frame that led me to believe that I would always have to do more, to get what I wanted, even if it meant using what I had; *what I had was me*. I grew up very fast and I was unaware that I was doing so. I wish that someone would've shook me and told me that I was doing it wrong.

I thought that for some reason I was special, and that GOD wouldn't allow me to be subjected to the harsh realities of having sex, but as you recall, he made an example out of me at age 14. My grandmother took my sister and I for our first pap smear; the visit was extremely uncomfortable and demeaning. After they explained the possibilities of potential diseases, I prayed that my results would come back clear. I literally prayed every day until they finally called. I was sitting at the kitchen table on what seemed to be a normal day. The sun beamed in on my skin and bounced rays into the distance of thin air. The phone rang and suddenly silence filled the entire house.

My grandmother relayed to me that they found a spot on my uterus; it was chlamydia. I didn't know what this

I am Porcelain

meant but I knew that it must've been a horrible thing. I was mortified and at a loss for words and so was she. Suddenly that sunlight turned into mountains of confusion. This was the first time that I possibly broke my grandmother's heart. Meanwhile, my sister's vagina got off scot-free. She was sexually active but not as early as I was, and she was much more careful with her body. My grandmother instructed me to write down my sexual partner(s). I didn't know what to say or do, so I just cried. I had been with only GOD knows who and it was all a secret, *until then.* Prior to my pap smear, I was in a relationship with an upper classman, in which I was crazy about. I didn't feel comfortable telling him because although he was very cute, he was also very childish. I knew that he would tell everyone that I gave it to him when in reality, I gathered that he must've given it to me. He was always bragging about how many girls he had been with.

  I handed my grandmother a piece of paper and hoped that the names would disappear before she touched it, they didn't. She looked at the list and could only manage to say *"Brittiny."* Knots form in my throat as I type this. I hated hurting her. She raised me and she thought that I was her innocent little girl; my list showed her otherwise. When I returned to school, I steered clear of all boys. My secret ate

I am Porcelain

me alive. I felt as though boys could smell that I had it or something and that they'd run from me because of it. While walking in the hallways of my high school, I imagined myself as invisible. I tried to walk fast and keep my head down. I felt doomed even though the STD was curable. There was this one boy who really liked me, and I liked him too, but I felt obligated to tell him that I had Chlamydia if we dated, so, I ran from him. I ran from him for so long that we didn't get the chance to date, but it saved me some embarrassment. After I got rid of it, I still couldn't stay away from what boys had to offer.

In most cases, boys only had one thing to offer but as I got older, I begged to differ. One of my closest friends had an older cousin who was absolutely "taken" by me, he loved my body. I took his lust with a grain of salt, until he offered me something for it one day. He texted me to tell me that he had just bought a new house, and that it needed to be cleaned because there were shoes, clothes, and miscellaneous items everywhere. He then asked me if he could pay me to clean it, the catch was that he wanted for me to complete this task in my bra and panties; I declined. I resided in a two-bedroom apartment with my siblings, mother, and grandparents. Shortly after I declined, I walked to the living room and overheard my mother and grandmother discussing funds for

I am Porcelain

food, I recall my grandmother stating that she needed more money. I stood there in place for a bit and then paced for a second, I decided to let him know that I would do it, but that he'd have to pay me upfront so that my grandmother could feed my siblings; he arrived with no hesitation and money in hand. I gave my grandmother the money and I told her that I'd be back and that I'd have more. I'm sure that you all are aware that everything doesn't go as planned; I quickly found myself in quite the predicament.

    We approached his home, I took a deep breath and entered with the intent of rushing through the embarrassment of what I had just signed up for. Oddly, the house wasn't in much disarray (RED FLAG). I continued to observe everything until I made it to his room. I found a corner and quickly stripped myself of all but my undergarments as he laid there watching me. I trusted him and certainly considered him to be friend. However, as I began to clean, he decided to offer me an extra hundred to finish the job... stark naked (SECOND RED FLAG); he received a hard NO from me. I laughed at the audacity of his efforts *(I smile and laugh when I'm nervous or uncomfortable)* while anxiously trying to hurry up I became uneasy. He remained lying on his bed fondling with drugs, in which was his profession, and also the reason that he could get a home at our age. I made it

I am Porcelain

to his closet but before I could finish, he grabbed me from behind and threw me onto his bed. This would've been more than okay, *if I actually liked him*, but I did not, and I had made that clear.

He was much heavier than I, there was no chance at getting up. He snatched my panties at every angle, licking and sucking in between my legs while I yelled and cried for him to let me go. I was pissed off and scared. This was unfamiliar dick. I did not want it to enter me. He had his other hand on my stomach, and he kept pushing me down. I used my hands to pry him off me as best as I could. He tried to calm me multiple times by saying *"I'm not trying to fuck,"* I wondered in that second what the hell he was trying to do then. I knocked his drugs off of the bed and anything else nearby. I screamed once more, he continued to suck and moan on my vagina- yes, I said suck. I was disgusted. I didn't know what else to do, so I stopped resisting, he then backed away. I eased away from the bed, drenched in his saliva. I snatched my clothes and put them on while demanding him to take me home. Who the fuck "mouth rapes" someone? I was shaken up for sure and my image of him was completely fucked. The ride home was silent. He handed me the rest of the money for cleaning, along with an extra hundred, I walked through the doors of my home rattled but okay. I saw

iBleedPoetry

I am Porcelain

my siblings eating, which made me feel good. I could've dwelled in what happened, but I knew that I would do it again because not only did I just seem to do dumb shit, I'd do anything for my family and for the right amount of money.

I wanted so much for my siblings because our mother wasn't very parental, she was more-so like our older sister after her husband passed away. He was gunned down by two men, when they took his life, *they took hers too.* While life did a number on my mother, my grandmother stepped up for all of her children. My mother was still very involved in our lives and loved us more than anything, but she was suffering mentally; I watched her become so feeble and so broken. I realize now that she wasn't meant to be a typical parent, she played different roles in our lives and we loved her for that.

My mother lived a very wild life, she believed in enjoying every aspect of what this world had to offer. Her partying became nonstop and so did her drinking; she was an alcoholic, just like her father. She and him both would come in late nights and early mornings, there was always a show. The kids and I would wait for our mother to come in because when did, she'd have bags of fast food; Jack in the Box was our favorite. We'd all sit up laughing, eating, and joking around while trying not to wake our grandmother.

I am Porcelain

    Eventually, I was old enough to party. Who better to party with than your own mother? At the age of 14, she took me to get my nose pierced. At 17, she spontaneously took me and my sisters to get our first tattoo. And before the age of 21, I had my first real alcoholic drink with her- which was Hennessy mixed with Tampico juice. The ride home was hilarious, she told me that I was a "happy drunk" while we were in the drive thru of our local Jack in the Box. My grandmother was not fond of my partying with her but when I was with her, she didn't drink, which was great for us all. She told me that she wouldn't drink because she felt that she needed to watch me. She was my best friend.

    There were so many wonderful moments and wild nights with my mother, imagine my heart when she left this world. I was on the verge of becoming an alcoholic, just like her. She was diagnosed with kidney failure; *the beginning of the end for her.* After that diagnosis, she was stamped with heart failure and suffered from many other health issues as well. Over time, she had two open heart surgeries, several mini strokes, and blood clots in which led to her death. Prior to this, she was operated on many times and was placed on life support more than anyone I knew, *but she always came back*; she was a warrior.

I am Porcelain

On July 20, 2014, one of my sisters found her in her hospital room with one leg and one arm out of the bed; almost as if she were trying to get up to inform them of what was happening to her. They didn't save my mother. She was alone. I can't even write these words without choking on lumps in my throat and tears in my eyes. Because of my bond with my grandmother, I always thought that I'd be fine if I lost my mother. I was not. I am not. Time did not heal; it just made the loss harder to believe.

Beauty was important to my mother. During her sickness, the color of her skin darkened, there was a port in her chest for dialysis that everyone could see, and her body swelled a lot due to missed treatments. She became very rebellious and unhappy with who she saw in the mirror, I never understood how traumatic this could've been for her *until now*.

Although my mother lived a very wild and courageous life, it came with some baggage, damage, and heartache that could not be undone. I wanted so badly for her to be happy before she left this world. I still wonder if she was. Ten days before she passed away, I received the first copy of *The Naked Truth*; my very first book. My mother and I hadn't been speaking, but GOD brought me to Arlington Memorial to ensure that I saw her one last time.

I am Porcelain

My little sister in which occupied the hospital room with our mother a guest, had gone blind and was rushed to the ER a few levels below. I arrived shortly after receiving the news and spoke to a doctor. He informed me that her going blind was due to the stress of our mother's health. My mother had been battling a lot, but blood clots were the current concern; if one went the wrong way… her life as we knew it… would come to an end.

On July 11, I walked into her hospital room with tension but left overjoyed to finally see her happy with me again. She and I were able to laugh and cry one last time. When my sister regained her eyesight, I walked her back to the hospital room with our mom. A nurse was there so I remained quiet and kept my head down; I felt so out-of-place. My mother didn't say anything to me when I entered, as I stated, we weren't speaking at the time. We were two in the same; wild, adventurous, and stubborn as hell. I didn't say anything either. She was upset because we (her children) didn't visit as often as we used to. It made me upset that she felt this way because I had begun working full time, I had new responsibilities, and I was trying my hardest to chase my dream as a writer. I was working on my first book and also attending open mic nights at different venues to perform Spoken Word Poetry of mine, for exposure; I wanted to

I am Porcelain

conquer *something*. I wanted her to be proud of me because she used to chase dreams too. I had always been there for her no matter what but when I grew tired and busy, she didn't understand. I am forced to grasp why now, she was lonely. She just wanted to see us more. I regret that I wasn't there.

I walked over to her bed eventually and handed her the Author copy of my book, without implying that it was mine. She looked at it casually, and then flipped it over, all to see that it was me on the back. Her energy shifted from a spoiled girl to proud mother.

"MY BABY WROTE A BOOK!" broke the ice and I could breathe again. I laughed as she continued to repeat herself. *"MY BABY WROTE A BOOK! SHE WROTE A MOTHERFUCKING BOOK,"* the nurse laughed too. I couldn't do anything but laugh and nod. I stood there in awe, watching her stare and analyze my creation; she was so proud. As tears took over, I told her not to cry and I wiped her face while telling her that we had some *"turning up"* to do. I sure did believe that we did, and I'd give anything to have this moment back. I used to write my mother letters when we'd have disagreements. I hadn't written a letter this time, but I did have an acknowledgement that I wrote specifically to her in my book.

I am Porcelain

I opened it, it read *"One of the greatest friends that I've ever had and the toughest survivor that I know, Kimberly Rochelle Hubbard. Throughout every illness and downfall, she remained beautiful even if she didn't believe it. I know that she carries pain in her heart for all that she has been through so as her daughter, I have a commitment within myself to help free her from that pain. There were times when I had no one to confide in; she was there for me. I have told her things that most of my friends could NEVER tell their mothers, so I honor her for that. I love my mother dearly. I partied with her at all times of the night, we're more like sisters; best friends. I wouldn't trade those moments for anything. Some would say that our relationship should have been strictly mother and daughter but forcing something like that would've only tainted the bond that we naturally had, so I appreciate being able to experience that part of her, because ever since she found out that she had kidney failure, she has been up and down the roller coaster of life. I have cried so many days and nights because I truly miss who she used to be. I wonder why this is happening and I can't provide any answer for myself, I just pray that she lives to see me make it, not just for me, but for the both of us."*

I looked up to see her face, all she could do was cry. She told me that she wanted her copy and that she had her money waiting on her debit card. She didn't even have to say that she was proud of me because I felt her admiration flowing through her veins and staring right into my face.

Losing my mother turned me into the angriest little girl in the world; I was hurt, broken, and bitter. I always felt that if I lost her, I would be alright, but truth is, her death took me to some pretty dark places; I wanted to walk through graveyards just to search for her presence. My partner thought that I was crazy. I didn't know how to handle her not being able to see me succeed and thrive in my biggest moments. I didn't know how to handle her not being here to witness my mistakes and cheer me on when I'm screwing up. I couldn't handle her not being here to be on my side, even if I was wrong. This is who my mother was to me. I could not fathom that pain. I spoke to my mother by phone on July 18, she wanted me to come to the hospital. I told her that I would come up there but that it would be on my off day, which was the 21st, it was a Monday. Monday came but she was gone. I feel like shit every time I think about it. I could not forgive myself.

I became so consumed with the death of my mother that I forgot about my grandmother. Once I realized this, I developed a massive amount of guilt. I should've grieved with her and been there for her because she had lost her child, her best friend, and her final daughter. My grandmother still continued to raise my siblings after she passed, and she's carried out that role to this day; we're all she has left. I began to do better at being there for her, as well as allowing her to feel okay to crumble, because we all need that.

My transparency in this tragedy, is for me to magnify the souls behind the stone wall; *the masks behind the makeup,* if you will. The moment that we sit our afflictions on the shelves of a vacant home, is the moment in which they decide to trail us out of the door we so anxiously ran from. Skeletons will form and they will dwell in our new homes to haunt us like ghosts until we make peace with them; until we make peace with ourselves.

Making peace with yourself could hurt; it could make your soul turn up at the sight of you. I've done some work. I was taught that if you are spreading your legs or constantly giving yourself away to someone, anyone, husband or not- they should be doing something for you. Many will not agree with this. But I did. I sold myself short by exposing myself to sex at such an early age. I now wonder if I diminished the image that I aspired to uphold. I wanted so badly to be the "good girl" and I'd love to portray that, but the truth is that I was very promiscuous. It took me years to admit this to myself. I used to collapse on the inside when I was questioned about men that I had slept with or the depths of my sexual activity; I was ashamed. If you feel or have felt the same way, then I'm sure that you've also felt that you are not a candidate for marriage or love. It's almost as if *we promiscuous girls* were counted out.

    In the black community, we tend to reject professional help. This is not healthy and it's not okay. So much for having each other's backs. Our mental health is so important. For instance, if we allow our pasts to determine whether or not we are capable of receiving love, we could potentially sabotage any man/woman that comes our way. It doesn't matter how many times the world tried to chew you up and spit you out, YOU are capable of being loved. You ARE loved. I used to think that it was okay to like that I was boisterous, devious, and a tad bit demented. I clearly needed help. I didn't receive counseling. Eventually, writing became the answer for me again; it was my way of healing. I have matured more due to the job that I currently possess, which is managing a caseload for special needs consumers. I don't have room to be nasty on the inside because I truly do possess a passion for people. For those of you whom are still straddling the fence in your own toxic ways, I suggest that you find a Counselor or a Psychologist because you will not be able to progress in life if your mind is not right. Try to

I am Porcelain

focus on merely being the best versions of yourselves. Focus on being genuine and let that light within your darkness, shine through. Imagine how much you will accomplish when you do. It took me a while to accept the things that I've done and to forgive myself. I believe that you can do the same.

Our minds conform to our surroundings which can either take us up or down. My mind has been a celebrity's mansion filled with books, secrets, dreams, lies, and fears. I try to get it all out of my head by orchestrating my thoughts on paper. When I first began to write, I was always in love, so I thought. My poetry was light and if it were a color, the color would be pink. As years began to pass, the color became black. The poems that I would write became explicit, rough, and vulgar. For the life of me I could not figure out why, then it hit me. My life was no longer light and pink, therefore my poetry, my thoughts, and my reality would not be either. I went from being *Perfect Patty to being Pinky (the Porn-Star);* now while my body count is nowhere near hers, I still had plenty to be ashamed of.

Sometimes we must question ourselves. We often question GOD (when we shouldn't) and people around us, but never ourselves. I shamed men, my father, my mother, and then shamed myself, but I had to figure out where I had gone wrong. I believe that I found an answer one night when

I am Porcelain

I was out with this overgrown ass man. I was of age, but he was much older. Any who, I lost my cell phone and asked him to use his cell to call mine. I glanced at his screen and saw that my name was programmed under a guy's name! What in the entire fuck, right? I think my name was "Greg." HA! I gathered myself in that very moment. I told myself that I was a woman and that my name is *Brittiny*. That day was life altering because I just KNEW that I would be avenging those hurt feelings of mine. Of course, you'd like to know what I did, nothing major, I just started sexing somebody else.

    I also adapted to the idea that women can do exactly what's tolerable for a man. I was informed that I shouldn't operate in this manner, but they had me sadly mistaken. *They* as in men. I tampered with doubled standards and initiated sex with whom I wanted to, when I wanted to. I had different guys for different things. I found it quite delightful to tear apart relationships. I felt that everyone would be happier single. I often still believe this. It's no wonder that I run at the first sight of conflict. I do not like to compromise, and I do not like to talk about issues; I have become the stereotypical man. I also lack compassion in my relationship, so I am still working on myself. The goal isn't to be perfect; the goal is to get to the root of our problematic selves.

I am Porcelain

A major issue is lacking self-love. We as women solely feel unworthy of all things good sometimes. There are a lot of movies that incorporate jokes to depict the realities of fatherless children. Every time I am confronted with it, I want to call the producer to tell them to stop making a mockery of us.

Most of the time, *girls become promiscuous because Daddy wasn't there to run the boys away.*
They become weak *because Daddy didn't show them HOW a man is supposed to love them.*
He didn't chase their pain away or tell them that their body is a temple.
He didn't put fear in the hearts of men who raised their hands to women.
Wasn't there when baby girl was raped or molested by someone in the family.
Daddy wasn't there.
And yet, so many people are humored by this.
I am all for a laugh but not at the expense of a broken daughter.
We're all just trying to find our way.

I am Porcelain; The Naked Truth

Dipped in Poison.

I am Porcelain

Tainted Hearts

We've talked about quite a bit so far. I am glad to still have you here with me. Let me ask you a question. Have you ever experienced butterflies floating within your existence? Did they make you feel clumsy, bashful, or even afraid? If so, that my friend, is the beginning of love.

Love is often confused with gifts, flowers, and romance. It's perceived as though whom we love, ought to be perfect; they are allotted zero mistakes and they can't do anything wrong, otherwise, they don't love us. I'm unsure of where the details of that fairy tale came from, but love is supposed to be a powerful thing; a unity, unlikely to bend when tragedy arises. A force to be reckoned with. Love. Love is supposed to be something that is trained to defeat various situations, such as affairs, lies, layoffs, and hurt feelings. I am not saying that one must undergo these experiences in order to have proof of said love. However, obtaining a relationship with someone involves many different stages; heartaches and hardships being one of them.

We witness various kinds of relationships, some people, maybe your parents or grandparents, have been married twenty + years. How? We are kept in the dark

I am Porcelain

regarding the fixes of these glorified relationships; maybe if we knew, we too could possess relationships with longevity. If you think about it, we were set up for failure. The only examples that we have are divorces due to cheating on either party, flakiness when times get hard, betrayal that soon leads to breaking up, and staying when you should leave. *We grew up and became these examples.* We became incapable of forgiving one another, and we move on too quickly before the dust even settles.

    My mother was the type of gal that took shit from no one. She would leave you in a heartbeat and have another suitor at the door in minutes, *if she saw fit.* If she so much as suspected any foul play in her relationship, she would begin to dabble in foul play of her own or end things immediately. I became the same way. The same ruthlessness, the same disregard for any potential explanations; I'D BE DONE. Absolutely OVER IT and I wouldn't shed a tear. My grandmother on the other hand, was a lover and lot of crazy. My grandfather put her through hell, but she was always there, and I never understood why. When she'd suspect wrongdoing on his end, she'd still have his dinner ready, habits (beer, cigarettes, snacks) available, and laundry washed and ironed; she remained a great woman. I questioned her why all the time, and she'd tell me *"You gotta learn to forgive Brittiny."* Now, don't get me wrong, my grandmother had her days of damn near killing him, literally, but GOD continued to guide her heart. To this day, they are separated but she remains that same sweet woman to him.

I recall being extremely young at the time, I wondered if forgiveness was worth the pain. I soon learned that forgiveness was for me and not the other person, but it was still very hard to do. Aside from encountering mishaps of my own, it'd be fair to say that I experienced a LOT of love. In my adolescent years, every guy that I met, I believed that he and I would be together forever, *which is hilarious upon reflection,* but needless to say, I was wrong.

Boys and men became more and more temporary because I used them in the same ways that they used me and every other girl in the world. It helped for a little while but eventually, it became my downfall. Whether I'd like to admit it or not, I ripped the backbones from people who loved me most because I was wasn't programmed to forgive. Majority of the women in my life were successful and driven, but single, so when I imagined myself taking those strides to become successful, I only saw *myself.*

I contemplated on several occasions if I should alter my mind frame. I love the idea of marriage and relationships with longevity, but I can't help but to feel that I am not built for either one. Leave it to my partner, I just don't like to compromise, which is true. I like the convenience of not being obligated to answer questions, argue, or include anyone in my decisions. Regardless of those imperfections, I have always been a sucker for love. I used to enjoy my mind scurrying to cloud 9 when I met somebody new. I melted when I was thought about and I craved the sexual vibes; I lived for it all. I should have been focusing on my career path, but I was troubled due to the fear of feeling alone; I wanted to have somebody, anybody.

  I encountered many situations and I created bonds with potential candidates, but nothing ever lasted long enough. I was intelligent, still very young, and naïve. I was lied to and strung along, but I still couldn't help but to genuinely see the best in them all. Eventually, I became irritable with the commonality of their actions- I assumed their gestures derived from a Mac Daddy handbook of some sort. I started changing, growing, maturing, and I liked it. I became aware of their truths and lies before they spoke them and then suddenly, my clay morphed from the various colors to the boldest blacks and darkest reds ever to exist. My shield said to love me or leave me the hell alone.

  I had a major crush on this boy in middle school, we always ran into each other during passing period and

I am Porcelain

afterschool. We became a couple soon after, I loved him. He was at my beck and call for anything that I wanted, and he walked from miles and miles away, just to see me. I was in the sixth grade; he was in the eighth. We were together for a while, even after he went on to high school. He was the first boy to ever write me letters, buy me flowers, gifts, and lunch at school. He was also very talented, so, he drew pictures and painted art for me often. He'd also compile lots of my favorite songs to make me CDs because I LOVED music. *I lost my virginity to him.* My mother wanted to kill him when she found out. I remember her staring fire into the pits of his soul. Nevertheless, we were inseparable and even when I ended it, he still treated me as though nothing had changed. It's still nice to know that he didn't use me or prey on me. I hurt him when I moved on.

    I apparently wanted to date even older guys. He was careful with me, but I wasn't with him. I guess that's why two years later, he began to date this girl that I thought was my friend. Everyone around me knew but never told me. I just so happened to have a simple dream of him with her, cruising through a yard on a lawn mower- *super random.* While at my former school, sitting on the bleachers during a basketball game, I laughed and told my best friend about it. She wasn't laughing. She said, "I thought you knew" and I

I am Porcelain

was like "KNEW WHAT?!"- imagine my surprise. This boy still showed up for me, rubbed my feet, bought me food and gifts with no sex what-so-ever, but was with someone else. Someone who was trying to be my friend. I was baffled but I knew that he still loved me and that he always would. I was upset but not for long. *Mad for what? Right.* My best friend told me that this girl told her that she had asked my permission before dating him, *which was a lie*, but it was all good. The love that he and I still had for one another was mutual, but I leveled up and never looked back again.

    I continued to date but this time, I wanted to have some fun. It was the summer before our freshman year in High School. The My twin sister and I got on a chatline one night and surprisingly met a couple of boys. We used to do pranks on the men, unless we ran into someone to our liking. The guys that we met were best friends, both extremely funny and cool. In the midst of flirting, we exchanged numbers. We both chose a boy and talked on the phone with them all night; we hit it off. I liked my boy so much and although he felt uneasy with my age, he agreed that he liked me too. He was in the 11th or 12th grade and again, I was barely a Freshman. We both had dancing in common; we'd dance until our bodies started talking. We also loved singing and writing music, we were very passionate beings. It seemed to be that we had so much in common. We met up and began the first stage of dating; we were adorable. We took professional photos at the mall, *that was the thing to do back then.* We met each other's parents and spoke far into the future about plans and endeavors. *Gullible much?*

The first day of school came, I wasn't prepared for what was about to take place. We set eyes on each other in the crowd of kids, I was excited, but I felt as though he were ashamed of me, in turn, I became ashamed of myself. I didn't have the designer clothing and shoes that he and his crowd had; he put the POP in POPular. However, he liked me before this day. So, I thought. Any who, He wrote me a letter and broke up with me the first day of school, from what I can recall. I was crushed and then to add insult to injury, I saw a potential reason as to why. I knew that he liked me a lot but in comparison to his ex-girlfriend, I was nothing. She was much older, dressed better, wore her own hair, and carried herself in a classy manner; it hurt. I saw her with him soon after he broke my heart. He was the first guy to ever break up with me.

As I became more confident, I fucked more and cared less. She was the nice church-girl type and me, I loved GOD too, but I also loved to party. He and I always ran into one another at clubs or house parties. After bumping and

I am Porcelain

grinding on dance floors, we eventually began to date again. To my surprise, I never had sex with him. Mainly because he had already proven that he was capable of breaking my heart, but we still had this crazy cosmic connection; undeniably one of the most emotional relationships I've ever had.

    He was later engaged to the girl that he dumped me for, but it didn't stop him from licking up my thighs at a party he saw me at soon-after. He never married her. I guess he saw how boring she was too. Believe it or not, her mother had the nerve to approach me on the grounds of our high school. She called me "fast" and gave me a piece of her mind, in which I could've lived without. She was wrong about me. I wanted to tell her that it was her daughter who was giving it up, but I didn't. I allowed her to think that she knew what she was talking about. For some reason, I felt the need to "respect the code." I did however contact my ex to let him know that it wouldn't be tolerated again. He was apologetic and thankful for me not sharing that tea. We remained friends and actually became closer during the transition of my adulthood. He and I would discuss the matters of new relationships and hang out as though we were best friends. We confided in each other and still never had sex. I never told him that he made me feel ashamed of myself

I am Porcelain

way back when, would it have been important to do so? I think that closure is important. If you have someone that made an impact on your life in such a way, then get your closure. Be clear that expressing your pain is not to rekindle but to rebuild from there.

    Boys, men, and everything in between, fail to realize that the ways in which they treat women, girls, and young ladies, mold the scope for who we will become. I reflect on so many encounters of what I presumed to be love and I feel so frustrated with myself. Why must we subject ourselves to the insecurities of others? True, I didn't have much but when I learned the trends and could afford to be different, I did with it what I could; I became my own person. A lot of times, it's not that people can't afford "what's hot" it's that they don't know about it. Introduce others to your world and allow them to choose.

    Although I feel that I was a pleasant person to be around, I see the distasteful sides to myself now. I became a daring woman after I settled into *me*. Was that the best that I could do with my character back then? We could blame it on my age, but I knew better, and I liked the thrill. So much so, that I dived into many relationships soon after. *Did I fail to mention that I cannot swim?*

I am Porcelain

Every relationship started the same. There was a course of three months in which we'd either become completely infatuated with one another, or we'd realize that it's not going to work out. Some of us ignore those signs and we force ourselves into relationships that are not beneficial to us. We have this misconception that if we love someone, then we must be with them; not true. I must say this aloud for those of you whom are tethering yourselves to toxic, abusive, and manipulative partners. Do not subject yourselves to foolery for love. Honor your hearts; *who told you that you couldn't love and let go?*

I foresaw an abusive relationship with someone in which I was CRAZY about. I did not want to pay attention to the signs, but they were always there. First, he wanted to control my money, then my phone, and then my voice. On Valentine's Day, he showed me his true colors; he punched me in my right leg during an altercation. The spot in where he hit me turned colors, and so did I- after I was done crying. I moved on. We were together for a nice amount of time, but I had to love him from afar. I learned that he was a bully and that he had been blinding me with his mask all along; which is why I was grateful for other relationships in my life. He was sweet and perfect in many ways, but in many ways, he was not. You must be able to differentiate between the two.

I am Porcelain

Well I'll be damned; *I've done a lot of dating.* Don't you wish that I could just drop some names? Unfortunately, I cannot. However, I can drop a reality check. Are you ready to cash it?

I used to be a great runner before I gained weight. I could run from my grandmother's home to a corner store in what felt like seconds. She'd always send me. It would take me forever to get ready because I prided myself on how I looked in public, but when I was finished, I would be gone and then right back with what she asked me for. She'd be so amazed, she'd say *"Damn girl, what you do? Run?"* and I'd laugh and say *"Yes."*

Well I guess you could say that's what happened when I accepted a proposal from whom was supposed to be my husband. I can appreciate that relationship because it was my longest relationship before now. We ended badly but after things cooled off, I told him that he was a good man, he just wasn't the man for me. Each day that I woke up to him was a surprise.

During the course of me recovering from the child that I miscarried of his, I bled for six or more weeks. I realized who he was during this time. I had never bled this long in my life, I felt as though I were dying. He would help me to the bathroom to clean me and change my pads, with

I am Porcelain

no remarks of disgust. I had to put huge under- pads on the bed because I was bleeding through everything. I would be so embarrassed, but he'd always express his respect for what I was going through. Not many men could do this, it was admirable. I truly did love him because I knew that he would always be there for me. He'd stare at me and wish that he could do something more to take my pain away. *That was love.* I may have never been sure about a lot of guys, but with him, I was certain. He even tried to get into the operating room when I had my DNC, but he was not allowed, per their protocol; so, he went to the hospital's gift shop and returned with gifts. He was always thoughtful like that and went great lengths to prove his love for me, but I ran from him the way that I ran to the corner store for my grandmother. Do you see yourself in this same predicament? Look into that. Now is the time to understand your actions.

  I miss my youth; a time that I can never return to. I recall being 15 and being in love with this guy that I met at a skating rink. Adults never take puppy love seriously, but something burned in my heart, mind, and soul for this boy. He was 19 and a senior, I attended his prom. I'm glad for that experience because I never had an opportunity to attend my own. I felt like Cinderella that night; he and my loved ones saw to that. We both enjoyed dancing too. He treated

I am Porcelain

me very well; he was first guy to take me out on real dates. We went to the movies often and to the mall to shop; he was the first boy to splurge on me. We were almost… something, but life happened. I began to rebel, and it was all over. He broke my heart in a way that I hadn't quite encountered before. I was always the one to break things off in any relationship that I had *(except one),* but not this time. Life was always happening, but I never saw it happening to us. We were tragically romantic. I will always cherish that because being in love was safe back then, that's what I miss.

I miss the concept of love because it is severely diminished in today's world. It is truly sad to know that some will never have it. There are many layers to the timeline of my life; so much has transpired. It may seem to be that I've grown into this wonderful woman, but I am definitely not her, not yet. I want to be admired for the steps that I've taken to gain control of my self-esteem and humanity, but not more than what I deserve because I am still struggling, just like you. We are all imperfect and afraid of what we don't allow ourselves to understand. I encourage you to grasp yourself some truth today. Find it and stand in it until you find the bliss that you've been longing for.

My truth is that I lack the capability to let go, but as I write to you, I realize that I have won because I am conquering something in this very moment. Love is a battle in which presented itself many times, but no matter how much I mess up, I am never too broken to love again.

Vulnerability is a door that introduces us to accepting emotions that we wouldn't normally be susceptible to. This state of being may be viewed as a weakness because it can cause us to make very dramatic decisions. What we forget is that being vulnerable can also allow us to feel what we are supposed to feel in that moment. It's okay to bend at the knee sometimes, even though you're used to standing; it's okay to be fragile. The journey is simply figuring out who you can be fragile with.

There are moments where you may need a hug, a kiss, or some passion, but you have nobody but a stranger in your midst, giving you the eye. If those looks lead to you in a bathroom pinned against the wall, then by all means, CHEERS to you and your climax. *We just need to get what we need to get sometimes, even if for only a moment.*

Being in a relationship with a woman now has been different. Our relationship is more intense than anyone I've ever been with. When I pursued her, I felt love for her in my stomach, in my eyes, in between my thighs, and more importantly, within the rhythm of my beating heart. I learned what chills were when I met her. I never knew whether to

I am Porcelain

open my eyes or my legs; it was a high that was not for sale. I did what I did best and dived in. *She has been my lifeguard ever since.*

She has shown me what it means to truly save something for myself. She reminds me that my past shall have no contribution to my dignity. I've learned a greater self-worth from being with her. *We are women.* We are women who love one another. Connected is what we are.

People have been so cruel to her and to us as a whole, which made me latch onto her even more. So, love who you love and hope that it all turns out in your best interest. *Keep the pain, keep the sorrow but never forget to keep the love.*

I am Porcelain

Reflections

I am Porcelain

I am Porcelain; The Naked Truth

Let me clear my throat.

I am Porcelain

Fan Favorites

I am Porcelain

1. <u>I Had my Husband's Mistress</u>

It was late, and I was sitting in front of the TV watching

"Love Jones," and I began to remember the love we had.

Guess you could call it my pity party, but I can promise you that it's not so bad.

I really miss those warm nights when you held me closely in your arms,

but my intentions are not to make you think that I wish I still had you, so, no need to be alarmed.

I just wonder what it is that I did so wrong.

So, think back to February 14th in the third year that we dated, but think hard.

If you remember correctly,

I spent that day and night alone and I hated it, but it doesn't even begin to compliment my scars.

I followed you to witness what was more important than me.

Standing in front of a hotel window my heart began to bleed. Allowing me to see that the bond of love that I

I am Porcelain

thought we still possessed, was diminishing right before my eyes.

Until that very moment, it was then that I knew, I was deeply barricaded in your lies,

but by surprise I didn't leave.

My feet were firmly rooted into the ground and the gap in my chest didn't allow me to breathe.

I marveled at the way that you caressed her skin, and the way that you undressed this woman.

I felt so betrayed, so replaced, that a stalker was what I was becoming.

I noticed the activity being displayed; it wasn't at all new.

I realized that everything you did to her, was what I had taught to you.

You grabbed this woman by her hair and gave her MY all.

I fell to my knees, mouth wide open because I didn't understand our fall.

Where is the consideration?

What happened to only wanting me?

I am Porcelain

Oh, the anticipation, and let's not forget the ring, you promised.

From the moment I laid my mind on pursuing you, I was never dishonest.

So, I checked into the same room, moments after you left.

I desperately rolled between the sheets and inhaled your scent, as I made love to myself; but, smelling her perfume quickly rectified my illusion.

I laid there motionless, trying to answer my confusion and I began to reminisce again.

I remember when you used to come home, I remember when I was your best friend.

Your presence gets me so high; I just wish that I could roll you up and smoke you all day and take you to bed with me when I sleep.

It didn't rub me well that she was reaping the benefits of the project that I put my time into, but in this world, I know that we don't play for keeps;

so, in this situation I did something that most women would never do.

I am Porcelain

I not only confronted the woman, but I took from her what I gave to you.

I bet you're wondering what I mean.

You see I just wanted you love me like you love your money and your name brand shoes.

Love me like a reporter loves to hear good news and kiss me.

Kiss me like you kiss your car or your paycheck.

You think I'm bitching now but truth is, I haven't even started yet. All I wanted was for you to treat me like a real man treats his mother, or just anybody he loves.

I needed you to cherish me like nature does the white dove, but clearly-

you will never grasp the concept of what it is that

I'm trying to say.

I guess this is the part where I tell you that, I fucked your mistress the night after that day.

I don't care that you returned after you were done playing around. That's why I packed you up nicely, because me and her are together now.

I am Porcelain

And besides, you only came back because you ran out of tricks for what you thought was your treat.

You make me sick, there's the door, I'm done with all the lies and the deceit.

Could you possibly be upset that I took what you hid from me?

I found her and told her that I was tired of you playing games.

I confessed that I watched you both make love, as I cried behind the windowpane in pain, and that's when she agreed that things needed to change.

But I believe I won her over the second I said, when you were making her cum, she should've been calling my name-

because if you analyze where you learned your sexual techniques, you'll admit,

I taught you all that you know.

So, I don't feel a bit saddened that I went behind your back and took your hoe.

But here's some advice,

time will heal all wounds if you let it.

I am Porcelain

But it's all good on my end hell, I just wanted my damn credit.

I am Porcelain

2. <u>BITCH was the title that they gave me</u>

They say you can't stay hot for too long, so I keep the oven lit, and heated under my ass to reassure myself that the temperature will rise.

I can enjoy the fame for however long it lasts; any outcome for me will be no surprise.

I'm just as cocky as the species with a penis, because my lyrics fly past your face faster than you ever could've seen it.

Been around to know that when I'm disrespected to always speak my peace.

You would say I'm too blunt; my mouth is slicker than these hoes in the streets.

AND BITCH WAS THE TITLE THAT THEY GAVE ME.

Sometimes I walk with my head down to keep from staring bullshit in the eyes.

Maintaining a smile instead of a frown, because I'm used to hearing so many lies.

Yea you could say I'm known for calling you out.

iBleedPoetry

I am Porcelain

I speak the truth for you because I believe even you don't know what you're about.

Standing on street corners hollering "Aye lil mama"

I throw my hand up and keep it moving because I don't have time for the drama.

Hearing about your baby mamas and how you can't pay your bills on time.

You want me to move in with you so that suddenly your problems can problems become mine?

AND BITCH WAS THE TITLE THAT THEY GAVE ME.

Intelligence and bearing the ignorance of men is what I truly possess.

So, when you come in at all hours of the night and I'm packing my bags, I bet you'll confess…

to the chick that you slept with in V.I.P. before you came back to me and brought H.I.V.

She's currently filing rape charges; did you see her I.D?

Foul situations are what it takes for you to realize who you've hurt.

I am Porcelain

Your life is suddenly flashing in front of your eyes and you can't even tell me what it was worth.

Legs wide open as you're eating your desert, when five seconds ago, it started off as just a flirt.

AND BITCH WAS THE TITLE THAT THEY GAVE ME.

Half of you niggas wouldn't know RESPECT, even if it rode your dicks every night!

We cater, cook, and clean, yet you still can' treat us right.

Out here trying to fight to be your wife, your mistress, and your playboy bunny.

At home sweating and slaving, while you out at strip clubs spending up all of our money.

It's that- or you're fucking our best friends, but once payback comes into the picture that's where the double standard begins.

The shit never ends…

"Oh, be a lady" they say.

"Don't let the pain he caused allow you to act this way."

Fuck you and society's brainwashing beliefs and opinions.

I am Porcelain

I'll take him, you and them and turn you all into my minions.

AND BITCH WAS THE TITLE THAT THEY GAVE ME.

Must I mention that my presence is breath taking and you're bound to be hypnotized?

Overwhelmed and infatuated, for short, an angel in disguise.

Just because I don't allow you to stomp the grounds that carry my heart, soul, and spirit-

as strange as it sounds, I never plan to let you near it.

I'm sweeter than the good pussy you've always planned to eat.

Don't fixate your mind frame on me because Ima always bring the heat.

I repeat-

Going harder than concrete, simple minded individuals will never have me beat.

The shit I spit is tighter than a straight man's asshole.

I'll rip out all of your intestines with a smile as I watch them slowly unfold.

I am Porcelain

And as they lay on the ground sitting harder than gold, I hold, the key to open up what you don't seem to understand.

I never needed you to set me free… raw and uncut…

BITCH- WAS THE TITLE THAT THEY GAVE ME.

I am Porcelain

3. *For My Mother*

I actually couldn't wait until this day because I would get to see your face.

Just so that I could hold onto one more memory for my heart and mind to embrace.

One more reason for me to believe that it's okay to die.

I could never fight back my tears but for you, mama I'll try.

My mother was a beautiful soul,

but my body rejects that statement as my words begin to grow cold.

I miss her now, but even when she was here, I still missed her for a while.

She stopped being herself a long time ago, there was too much pain behind her smile.

I can't believe she's gone.

I can still hear her laugh ringing in my ear from the day that we hung up the phone.

There was loneliness in her voice.

I was too caught up in going on Monday, sadly I wasn't given a choice, but

I am Porcelain

"I'll find a way to get through…

living without you."

Only God may know why he took you away from your nine kids.

I can't go against him because there was good reason for what he did, but we had so much more to do.

I prayed long and hard because I felt there was a point that WE had to prove; you always come back, but this time my heart shed to pieces.

You were pushed to your limit, I'm speechless.

I could write away my heart all night, but I still doubt that you can reach this.

We constantly told you that you were beautiful, even if you didn't look exactly the same.

You didn't believe it therefore it began to rain.

Now I'm lying in the bed trying to analyze this pain, blood boiling in my veins.

They say, I never quite pictured myself this way.

I'm scared, I don't know who I am today or if they'll continue to care.

I am Porcelain

I can't breathe.

I want to be brand new again but how do I fall to knees and I say God have mercy on them please, but what if it were me?

"Will you still love me when I'm not young and beautiful?"

Kim we still loved you, mama we still love you.

They say you're not suffering anymore but damn what about us?

Then again, I guess they're right.

I can hardly handle cramps.

Your pain was MORE than excruciating.

I'm talking heart surgeries, life support, and not to mention dialysis in which left your body aching; real pain.

Strokes, seizures, and blood clots, but what about living life on Earth without your soul mate because he made it to Heaven before you did, man that's a lot.

I couldn't have made it here this long.

Yet and still I want you to come back to me although I know that it's wrong.

I am indeed selfish.

I am Porcelain

I am trying to be strong but man I can't help this.

I am not wearing black for you; I'm wearing it for me-

because without you I am nothing but a withered flower,

a dying seed.

I am afraid to sleep knowing that you are gone.

I try to find sunshine "but it don't ever light the dark."

My mama left and didn't tell me that she was going.

What good is a final good-bye if you're the only one left knowing that you're leaving.

I'm trying to accept it, but I can't charge it to the game because it's all not worth believing.

Quotes derive from music; Brandy's song "Missing you," Lana Del Rey's "Young and Beautiful," and Lori Perry's "Up against the wind."

I do not own copyrights to this music.

4. *Favors*

Do me a favor and pretend as if my heart were an egg, and carry it with caution, so that it won't crack or break completely,

because once the mess is made, there's no way to clean it up easy, believe me.

For I am the illumination you've needed in all this darkness.

I will strike you harder than any match, so I dare you to try and spark this.

Watch me blaze you a flame brighter than any lighter.

You burn within my soul like hell as if I could even bear the fire.

You've tapped into my wants and needs satisfying my deepest desires.

Tell me, what will you require in order for me to love you hard and long?

I'm aware that I possess weak qualities, but I can assure you that I am strong.

I am Porcelain

How can I race the tracks of your past just to collect the dust and pray for its nonexistence?

Its bittersweet realities?

Are we going to linger behind and unwind exposure just to undress its fallacies?

Unanswered questions suddenly result to technicalities.

Must it be a crime that I just want you to swarm within me like honeybees?

Please just tickle me.

Make me laugh.

Whisper into my ear sweet nothings that my mouth could never give you back.

Please do me a favor and tie your soul to my chest so that when I breathe, we breathe together,

and so that every time my heart beats, you know it means forever.

Imagine that my lips are the only ones you're supposed to kiss or touch.

We all know there's plenty of fish in the sea, but I have to admit that I like the rush.

I am Porcelain

To know that you could be kissing anyone but you're kissing me.

You could be loving her but you're steady loving me.

I'm blinded with passion therefore I'm not allowed to see-

that this could end badly, but so can anything.

So, do me a favor and lie to me.

Tell me that you love me even if you don't.

My heart will always believe those words,

even though it's my mind that won't.

But keep lying to me,

because in it all I will hold onto your body as if it only possessed life because of me,

because of whom I am,

or whom I refuse to be.

Just keep lying to me because eventually… I will believe it.

5. <u>Slavery in Reverse</u>

Ever hear a soul screech from a line of fire?

Burning alive asking to be born again?

At what extent do you turn your head to have mercy?

Don't you think that for one eternity my soul will be forever be thirsty?

Masa I picked your cotton, and I witnessed you rape my wife; what more do you want from me?

I watched you lynch my brothers and sisters as the rocks that covered the ground scraped the skin from my knees.

I begged you "please" work me harder even though the blisters on my feet whispered for relief.

I am nothing but a slave to you… tired, black, and beat.

Where is your humanity?

Who taught you to be so cruel?

I believe that one day things will change, so for that-

you think I'm fool, and it hurts,

but I just want to know how you would feel if things were in reverse?"

I am Porcelain

Ironically that afternoon spirits flew from within the men and sent chills down their spines.

Neither one of them could see what was coming, guess you could say they were better off blind.

The slave woke up next to his master's wife, and breakfast in bed from one of his own.

He quickly jumped up and checked the mirror and asked to be alone.

"My skin is white, and I am living so well, tell me how could this be?

I am no longer a slave so my master must be me."

There is more than just poetry to this history, because you see-

Willie Lynch didn't discriminate when he planned our futures and calculated 300 years in terms of our "nigga behavior."

He demanded that slave owners test black women to see if they would submit to their dignities being waivered.

Talk about the abuse that women experience these days.

Their boyfriends, husbands, and fiancés –

I am Porcelain

strive to be their masters.

There's something terribly wrong with that picture but allow me to finish this story as my heart beats faster.

There was a screech from the plantation when the slave master woke up in sticks.

He had no clue what was going on, all he managed to say was "This is some bullshit."

Both men ran from opposite directions toward one another longing for an explanation.

Everyone grew worried because they were baffled by this observation.

"I'm you" the slave spat out.

"And I am you, what is the meaning of this?" Masa asked.

The slave glanced at his watch, smiled, and responded in a firm tone.

"You will be working the field today, but Masa you- will be alone, you should start now."

He told the slaves to take a day of rest.

Masa couldn't refuse because he'd suffer lashes across his chest.

I am Porcelain

"But my back is in so much pain, my feet are aching and it's about to rain.

I need food and-

"Oh, I remember a day where I said the same."

The slave master walked away and did what he was told.

Things were changing around the plantation but possessing so much power was getting old.

The days and nights were long, and he began to fall asleep.

He fell to his knees, as if suffering the worst disease, and he began to weep.

He was approached by two men with whips longer than the acres he owned.

The slave jogged over to his flesh, knowing that what was about to take place would be wrong.

He wanted him to pay, to show Masa all he didn't know.

From scars, death, and rape he was front row and center.

They didn't know how long this switch would last, but it'd be something they'd always remember.

I am Porcelain

The slave knew his master was familiar with death, rape, and long days, but he only knew those things as a man of power and not a slave.

He had the chance to beat him, take advantage of his wife, kill his brothers and sisters, or even him, but instead he whipped him with patience and understanding.

He beat him with empathy, although his anger was quite demanding; he was standing in a position of his own power.

The thought of getting even made his dick harder by the hour, but it was something that his integrity didn't allow him to devour.

He stared his master into the eyes and realized that he had just won.

Returning the favor of his life as a slave wouldn't make his victory any more fun.

Regardless of corruption he chose to forgive.

Blacks are considered "animals," but even WE know holding so much animosity is no way to live; we don't have to retaliate.

I am Porcelain

We can conduct ourselves properly without being filled with so much hate.

Even if there is a reason for it to be there in the first place.

I am Porcelain; The Naked Truth

She Spoke w/ Passion.

I am Porcelain

They say, "Sticks and stones may break my bones,
but words will never hurt me."

I just wanted to let you know that they lied to you.

-Britt.

I am Porcelain

6. *Betrayal at its Best*

Wrap me in your most inner emotions and bask in my existence.

For the only thing left to say is "Good-bye."

As I hold onto bittersweet memories, my soul won't allow me to cry, and in all this madness; you wonder why I'm leaving in the first place.

It couldn't have been a mistake that you can hardly remember our first date.

Not due to just forgetting, but much rather having too many because as far as women well, you've had plenty.

Not just in the midst of our separation, but while we were together.

So how you can you expect me to bond my life with yours forever?

I better stop right there, because the thought of being strong on my own is all that I can bear.

How is it that I suffer continuously when you were supposed to care?

iBleedPoetry

I am Porcelain

Every single night I spent alone, I wondered where you were.

Imagining the way you touched her like me was just something I didn't deserve, that's why I prefer- to vanish and remain in my own skin.

I expected to be involved in your surroundings and be someone in which you can depend on.

After five years of what I thought was love, I'm forced to be alone. Had I connected with my senses; I would've saw my sister's underwear.

I would've heard the moans and groans after experiencing that blank stare.

You know- the one where you start to feel guilty, but you proceed in doing bad deeds?

Strangled in confusion because you were supposed to be supplying my needs, instead- you were straddled dangerously in between her legs on my bed, permitting her to have access to your skills in "great head," guess this is where I became fed up.

Every other woman took the cake as well, but this right here was enough.

I am Porcelain

How I am to even look her in the face?

Knowing that it was her for three years in my mouth, I still can't believe the taste.

You never graduated college, so how is it that you have a degree in betrayal at its best?

And no, I'm not taking shots this is just a part of what's on my mind to confess.

I thought that I was blessed to have a man who loved me so much.

I didn't know for a long time that your intentions were corrupt- because you couldn't keep your dick in your pants.

I have officially become my own woman, so this is where I take my stand.

You saw how many men glared at me on the outings that we had.

I know that it would kill you to see me with anyone, but that's just too damn bad.

It's sad, because we could have had something good.

As I walk out this door, I know only then, that my point will finally be understood.

I am Porcelain

So, wrap me in your most inner emotions and bask in my existence, for the only thing left to say is "Good-bye."

I am Porcelain

7. <u>Never</u>

I never want to see you again.

I never want to see you again.

I never want to see you again because you made me do things that I would never do.

My heart convinced me that you loved me, but my mind told me that it was never true.

It was actually far away from the case.

See, all you ever wanted was to control me with cruel intent, punch me in the face, and slap me across the lips.

The ones I used to kiss you with, but there are more scars to count that decorate my hips from where you took me, and you took me, and you took me again.

I should have gone with my first mind because it told me to only be your friend.

As a result, it's my broken heart that fails to mend.

There was an outcome not worth the awakening, not worth the petty phone call, not worth the pain.

I am Porcelain

Even after all of your mistakes, I still waited for you to change, but let's not play the "blame game" because I played a part in this too.

I allowed you to numb my intelligence because I felt your sob stories were true but believe me when I say that I'm through.

I won't count the tears that fall from my face tonight, I'll count sheep instead.

I won't look for you to walk through the door because I no longer want or need you in my bed.

I never want to see you again.

I never want to see you again.

I never want to see you again but then again; I really hope that I do.

There was no closure, no explanation; I'm not sure what all is true.

Didn't you love me?

What about the days that I made you breakfast, lunch, and dinner?

How about the nights that I rode your man hood?

I am Porcelain

What else must I make you remember?

Oh baby, you had me caught up in this natural disaster.

I don't know whether to cry or be angry in our final chapter.

I'm invisible to what's seen and unseen.

Won't you please call me back and tell me what your actions were supposed to mean?

I thought that I gave you what you wanted or maybe I was too damn nice, too laid back.

I could've popped off if I wanted to but, I was trying to be much classier than that.

I never want to see you again.

I never want to see you again.

I never want to see you again because it took you three days to muster up the lies you told me over the phone.

I couldn't have caused this heartache; I didn't do anything wrong.

So, you don't want me anymore huh?

As much as I want to say, "well I don't want you either,"

I am Porcelain

I can't, my lips won't allow me to lie.

I could have any man that I wanted, but I'm fixed on you after a year and I don't know why-

why the sudden switch of emotions on your end?

You act as though it doesn't faze you now, but you will never see, taste, or smell me again.

I will lose your number, but you will lose your mind.

You've made me an angry black woman; no need to be kind.

I just thought that I'd tell you face to face that you are no longer a factor.

You are no longer a being that my heart will require me to look after.

I will love myself...

as if you never existed; as if you never even mattered.

My world will finally change because I am no longer your battered-

woman.

I never want to see you again.

8. <u>You</u>

You came back to me and I couldn't help but smile.

I thought that we would never part, but we did for a little while.

Then we repeated this game for a moment at a time.

Each moment was different, my heart began to unwind.

I sat back wondering why you did this to me, and now, I know.

What's confusing me at this point is, where do all of my feelings go?

I missed you,

I wanted you,

I loved you, how long will this last?

Is this confusion allowed to continue or will it keep position in your past?

I am forever waiting on you; it's always been you.

9. You Said

You took my love and you threw it all away.

You knew that I didn't believe you, when you said what you had to say.

I gave you my heart, but you left it broken and in pain.

You told me from the start that your leaving me was insane; I wonder what changed.

You said that you wanted me to be your wife.

Said that it'd be you holding me at night.

Said that you'd always be there.

Hugging me, kissing me; heart bare.

Said there'd be no more tears seeping through my shirt.

Said that you'd help me recognize my worth.

I spent nights alone thinking about how you betrayed me; you just had to screw up my head.

I'll never trust another man again... and it's all because of what you said.

10. Why Does He?

Why does he put himself into a position where in the end he has to lie?

Why after he finally confesses, HE feels the need to cry?

He couldn't possibly have any remorse for the betrayal; he played a part in your pain.

Why does he continue to ache your already broken heart, trying to fix things that will always remain the same?

Why does he think or feel that he can treat a woman like you right?

The only thing that he's good for is mistaking you for his whore; he can't even come home at night.

He's at a point in his life where he is set in his ways; he can't be a man.

Why does he even begin to convince you to believe that he can?

11. Reflections of My Past

You took away my sexuality.

Face smothered into your pillow;

I knew that God wasn't so proud of me.

You devoured my objection and regurgitated pure selfishness.

Reflecting on my strength, I couldn't fathom my helplessness.

I was drained and in this particular drought it rained… blood.

Crying and screaming hoping that my tears wouldn't over flood.

Was this the true consequence of thinking I was in love?

12.   *Fifty Shades of Fucked Up*

I bet you didn't know that I'm the type to walk right up to you, look you dead in the face, and tell you that I JUST want to fuck.

No long-term relationship goals here, but hey let's waste time, you can try your luck; but I get bored very fast.

For your sake you don't have to be a comedian; but you damn sure better know how to make me laugh.

You'll see some scratches and some scars resting on my thighs, but don't be alarmed this time, -

I promise I won't cry.

The memories of my past are just that; I will no longer live in regret.

You see, I've been programmed;

Programmed to fuck –

to forget.

I was supposed to fuck to forget the pain.

One day I hope that I forget to fuck,

maybe then that'll bring the rain.

I am Porcelain

I bare my darkest convictions, but I can't quite determine what made me so cold.

I'll be bad to you, and only in the worst way, as if my antics will never grow old.

But let's not confuse things, you can never hurt me more than I've ever hurt myself.

I've become acquainted, well acquainted with all the broken ways that I've felt.

I am shattered memories fading into the background.

I want to be in love but sometimes, I honestly just like the way that it sounds.

I bet.

I bet you didn't know that I fuck to forget.

I am Porcelain

13. <u>Mistaken</u>

Love is a word often taken for granted; hardly cherished.

One loves another more than the other, -

fighting for a marriage.

Forever and always subjected to tears and wrongdoing.

Lost within the feathers of the flock, nothing but despair left pursuing,

She's ruined and sadly…

mistaken.

14. *November*

As this month drew closer, I dreaded the reality of how I would really feel because I thought about you today.

I was nervous as if I was waiting for something, or as if something was waiting for me.

My brain is constipated with "what ifs" and it can't seem to release the truth; you're gone.

Right when we found out about you, we began to prepare for you a new home.

I knew that I was weak in so many ways but for you, baby I was strong.

I didn't feel alone, anymore.

I was for sure that around this time "motherhood" would be knocking at my door.

But here I sit in bed typing you a love letter,

hoping that the sky is relaying my messages; it's November.

I thought that I had been through enough my darling, but you were supposed to be here before December… 2012.

I was for sure that I would be fine but all of a sudden, I'm not doing so well.

I am Porcelain

I think I'm going crazy.

I started a new job two weeks ago and in my department all I see is babies... and pregnant women... buying maternity clothes...

Please tell me you're somewhere in my presence tattooing your birth date on my soul.

I will never forget you.

How could I ever move on?

The only way for me to cope is writing poetry, talking to God, and listening to sad songs.

I try my best not to give up, but everything seems so wrong; so out of place.

I rock back and forth, contemplating if I lost you on account of my own mistakes.

You changed my life the morning I knew of your existence.

I wanted that bond.

I wanted that love.

I wanted the ability to be your glove; your protection.

I wanted to always be there to share with you my knowledge and affection.

I am Porcelain

All of a sudden, I feel as if the roles have reversed because now, I'm the one in fetal position, waiting on some sort of development.

Crying only numbs the pain for a little while, but I'm not sure who's really hearing it.

Why did you leave me?

I would have been a wonderful mom although late nights become uneasy.

We would've made it through.

I guess it doesn't matter anymore because I'll never know what it means…

to have you.

15. *Sleepless Nights*

Blow me like leaves in the wind on a cloudy afternoon and display your love for me, as if it were for "show and tell."

I've spent nights trapped in the pits of your emotions, no longer recognizing what it means to burn in hell.

This spell that you have me under permits the aches in my heart to believe in the unexpected, so no matter how far you go, I'll never regret or forget it.

Completely beheaded; cut off from any future in tomorrow.

I look deeply into those wandering eyes and all I see is your sorrow, your story.

She said to me that if I wanted to find her, she'd be in the back of some man's van, kidnapped and on the way to the land of the unforgiving.

Foggy windows, burning souls, and tainted woes I know she hurts.
Time has passed tremendously yet she doesn't know her worth, I deserve…

to know who she was first, you know before she changed.

Before she was exposed to the bitter drops of rain, symbolizing pain.

I am Porcelain

I want to make sure I express this verbatim so that I do not mention her in vein.

I came to realize that she wasn't just a memory.

She wasn't just a lollipop being liked until nonexistence, she... was me.

I was the tears that left scars behind, painting imperfect pictures in which were no comparison to the Mona Lisa.

You couldn't buy, sell, or trade me online with master card or visa; cash only.

A child manipulated into believing that I couldn't survive being lonely.

I was just a baby.

I thought that I could let go of my past, but as I get older, it drives me crazy, maybe, what should be tucked away safely isn't so sacred.

Unfortunately, there is no clean slate after heavy drinking and getting faded.

I waited for you to save me.

Talk about a sleepless night.

I am Porcelain

16. *Mommy Loves You*

I tried to advertise happiness, but it deflected into pain.

I tried to open up my heart, but got the feeling there was nothing to gain.

As I lay in my bed troubled, I am in disbelief of my loss.

There is nothing I wouldn't have given to have you, and I mean that at any cost.

Every ache I had was unbearable, believe me it was terrible, but I smiled because I knew it was you.

It broke my heart to know you were really gone, there was so much that I wanted us to do.

This devastation- brings me to a halt; to a place of misunderstanding.

Where in my confusion I'm baffled because of all that I was planning.

Some say it'll be okay, and others reside in a loss as well.

I slowly try to pull myself away as I am mentally burning in this hell.

Sonograms, heartbeats, and every mother to be...

I am Porcelain

Rude awakening as my soul sinks…why were you taken away from me?

My bun in the oven.

My bundle of joy.

My seed.

Reflecting on this tragedy, you are really what I need.

A shock, that quickly turned into my destiny.

Tears of disappointments as destruction got the best of me.

I see… that God couldn't bear to allow his angel to walk this Earth.

Or maybe that's just what I need to believe, in order for my heart not to hurt.

Visions of who you are and pondering if your physical appearance is similar to mine.

I drown every moment in these thoughts refusing to ever leave you behind.

I pray that I meet you in Heaven and that you'll know who I am.

Until then say hi to Kevin for me, and let's not forget my Aunty Pam.

I am Porcelain

Find Mama and Papa and hug them really close.

And if you can, hug yourself, because saying these words hurt the most.

I am Porcelain

17. *Separations of Darkness*

I try, because it's better than not trying.

I live, because it's worth not dying.

But I'm crying inside; feeling the love from my Lord that is allowing me to stay alive.

While battles of destruction corrupt what it is that I have to hide.

Or could it be that it's just Satan toying away with my pride?

You can tell when a woman is sexually active, because she has pain wiped across her face.

Not always, but most of the time, it's an experience that we yield to embrace.

Once that moment of virginity fades away, our innocence does too.

Relaxing on reality, we fail to comprehend that this is in no way true.

It doesn't matter if you were married, promiscuous, or you only did it one time.

I am Porcelain

Sex comes with pleasure, emotions AND pain, you can't just leave it behind.

Consensual or not, something is taken away from you and you can never get it back.

Falling apart on the inside, you recognize that it's way more than just that.

Some will love you.

Some will go on to the next.

Some will stay… and others will try to own what you shared.

The selflessness, the way you cared… and at that very moment you're scared because you didn't think that it would happen to you.

How could a flower so beautiful, with petals so soft, wither up into nothing but a traumatic memory?

Suddenly the man you honored and loved has taken a front seat to forever being your enemy.

Every rip and tear that he caused has implanted insecurities, guilt, and an unforgettable train of thought.

Was it my fault? You ask.

I am Porcelain

Or should I have done more than just fought?

Reliving this experience, you are taunted by the ghost of a virgin girl, in which of whom you anticipated.

You find yourself ignoring this voice that's telling you that you should have waited.

At the same time, you hate it because you wish that you could've stood against the temptation.

So many people fall for seduction and any forms of sexual demonstration.

Going back to that very moment when you thought that you were safe.

Eyes opened or closed; you didn't think that you would be raped.

"No" you say-

"Stop" tugging away-

"Get OFF OF ME"-

He says, "Just relax" and "Let it happen, there's no way I'm setting you free."

Devouring your objection and disregarding your tears.

I am Porcelain

You lay there grabbing the sheets and you take it, as you come to grips that you are now living one of your biggest fears.

Legs kicking, fingers pinching his skin.

Face buried in his shoulder, hand, or a pillow,

you don't know where to begin.

Is it a skeleton in his closet?

Do you forgive and let go?

Do you think he's actually sorry?

How will you ever really know?

Covering up your ears, you want to believe that everyone means well.

It's that, or either you're considered to be naïve as hell.

Forgetting is what you plan to do but you can't block, delete file, or erase it.

It picks at your existence; the only thing you're forced to do is face it.

That's why I try, because it is better than not trying and I live, because it is worth not dying.

I am Porcelain

I'm relying on a source to occupy my elevation.

I'm involved in the separations… of darkness.

18. *Fatherless Child*

We live in stereotypes, so as I rock the mic, I just want to let you know that every girl without a father-

doesn't turn out to be a hoe.

Broken maybe.

You see he told me that he had been stealing hearts all of his life, but I didn't believe him until he stole mine.

That wasn't all that he snatched, but too bad he couldn't pay for this crime.

I thought I was in love.

I thought that he would hover the cells on my skin like a latex glove; close to the touch.

He had me yearning like crazy, I simply wanted him so much.

Lust shouldn't have been my only attraction, because it put me in situations where I only desired "the heat of the moment" reactions, and nothing more.

I accepted him cheating, beating, and creeping on me because I had nothing to want for.

He always came home.

I am Porcelain

It didn't matter that I heard another woman's voice every night he laid next to me, sweet talking on my phone.

I guess I just couldn't stand the thought of being alone.

I was crazy.

Crazy like crossing the street during rush hour or making love to electricity while enjoying emotional shock in the shower.

I was bleeding.

Instead of bleeding love I was dripping desperation, hoping that it would drain me dry.

I held hatred in for so long that I couldn't even afford to cry.

The damage was done.

He had a lock on me squeezing my soul tighter than vice grips.

I was so easily manipulated that I snapped faster than lays potato chips.

My hips favored the bruises that he painted on my skin.

Sad thing is after all of that, I still wanted to be more than friends.

I am Porcelain

I sprayed cologne on the pillow in which he slept on for the hours that he would disappear.

I wanted him to remember what I smelled like, so I worked him harder than I did my career.

The things a woman will do to be held at night.

The things a woman will do to be loved.

The things a woman will do to be touched, remembered, and taken care of.

I wish forgetting was just as easy as breathing, but sometimes taking a breath is the hardest thing to do when you feel like you're dying.

I experienced broken hearts and STDs way before my time,

I'm not lying-

if there is a time for that at all.

A fatherless child on a journey awaiting the tremendous fall.

I'm disconnected like past due services, and completely shut off like showtime curtains.

I needed to brush my past like teeth and hope that the wind would carry my skeletons beyond my feet.

I am Porcelain

I thought to myself, I am one messed up individual, but previous encounters convinced me that I wasn't the only one.

A new beginning begun, but the bones found their way back to me.

He was just like a nigga wanting me to close my mind and think with my legs.

So, I opened up cautiously and asked if he could fuck my brains instead.

That was something that he failed to do.

Eventually I moved forward with a different mind frame and found someone new.

No more different person every week.

No more wondering if he will love me tomorrow.

I get to wake up to the same man every morning and go to sleep with the same man every night.

I get to wake up and say, "good morning".

I get to wake up and remember his name,

and fall asleep knowing...

that he knows mine too.

19. <u>Why Does the Bruises of a Lover's Fist?</u>

Why do the bruises of a lover's fist strike a pose towards the only hope of nature, and wind down to the lifelessly and breathtaking chance of another world?

Sorrow, humiliation, and frustration broken down to smallest ounce of pain.

Stop the rain, hail, sleet, and snow.

Let me know about this "other life" with these people and places, all unfamiliar faces and mishaps.

I want to go above and beyond, am I wrong?

Well no.

Take me back and please let me start all over.

No red rover; side to side.

All forces of destruction left to hide and come out when the world is doing okay.

Not promising another day, life does us this way, and I'm sorry to say.

I wish there were another moment for me to steal and conquer; for it is I whom lights up this life and your world.

I am Porcelain

I'm your little girl.

I am the promising dream left to succeed.

Will I die without you? No.

Go poor without you? No.

Live better? Yes.

I think that's it-

because you're that piece of shit that goes round and round in this toilet, which is my life.

I've always wanted you to wake up and do us right.

I'll be damned to lose without a fight.

I was always wanting "daddy" to come in and tuck me in at night and tell me bedtime stories and say to me "I love you," but it's too late to step in now because the bruises of a lover's fist have struck again.

This time the bruise is an everlasting mistake, ruin, crime, and a felony.

These sweet words said to you my father is let out and has turned into a melody.

Now you feel my rage, my wrath, and my way of living at this point of emotion, you showed NO devotion.

I am Porcelain

I'm fine without you, but it hurts because I'm supposed to have you and be able to grab you and say "dad!!!"

Well it's nice to know what I should've had, and what every child with no father wants so damn bad.

There are no chemical reactions in this experiment that have devoured you yet, but there will be, and you'll see that it was me who brought on the pain and humiliation.

You'll live through and understand my demonstration, and the true meaning of empathy.

I'll never need or ask for your sympathy, but you'll know the way that I feel.

I thought this could be a dream but no daddy it's all real.

You're a murderer and you should do time for tearing apart the heart of a young, talented, intelligent, and beautiful young girl.

There's so much to describe me and what I would do to change this world.

First off, fathers, sperm donors, and "daddies" like you will feel the bruises of a lover's fist and taste the tears of a crying child with no father.

I am Porcelain

You'll be drinking for days, so don't even bother, but I'll help change those foolish and childish ways.

Let me expand the time and unwind a heart especially made for you and it goes like this…

"You left me once and I was way too young to understand why.

You left me twice; I knew and understood so I cried.

Then you left off and on, but the last time hurt the most.

I want you to get a dose of your own medicine!

That starts off with fessing the whole truth and telling me why you ran away from responsibility, and chance of a lifetime.

You make me sick, and I wouldn't dare want you as a father of mine.

You're stupid-

and I wish I never really knew you, because now all I do is think of you, and dream of you, and watch for you, and wait for you to come and take me under your wing to heal these bruises of a lover's fist.

Do they hurt?

I am Porcelain

Can you make it better?

Will they ever go away?"

I am Porcelain

20. *The Real Shit*

I sat on the kitchen floor with a knife making love to my hands.

I got this feeling in my gut that it was time for a master plan.

No more contemplating if this cut could suddenly devour my purpose here on Earth.

I just had to take the tears and pain, along with what it was worth.

Even though it hurt, I could feel my imagination and curiosity start to flirt as one, bringing me back to reality that a nightmare had just begun.

Rocking back and forth I placed the knife on different sections of my arm as I made a fist.

I then took it to another level, and I aimed it at my wrist.

Looking down I asked myself should I slit fast or dig deep, because at that moment the sound of death sure seemed sweet.

Not only did the thought of loved ones losing me and me losing them hold me back, it was more so fear.

I am Porcelain

All chocked up, tears running from their own home trying to figure out how the hell I got here, to this location.

How could this urge to destroy myself be my final destination?

Pause.

Suddenly teardrops of frustration overcame my happiness and continuously ran down my jaws.

I wish that I was back in the day waiting for Santa Claus,

Because that's when I never had to worry about what went on within these four walls.

Or maybe when I was just a baby still learning how to crawl.

Stop.

Pregnant with opportunity I could feel my dreams pop- like a bubble.

Someone was looking out, never looking in, saying there was going to be nothing but trouble.

I was preparing myself for the worst, everything functioning in my body wanted to burst.

I needed to get myself under control first.

I am Porcelain

Quit.

Struggling to give birth to this person from within, I was forced to deal with the real shit.

I am Porcelain

21. *The Kiss of Death*

I closed my eyes and welcomed death as if it had a gift for me.

The grim reaper didn't seem so scary after all.

It was like love at first sight, so I didn't mind the call.

He was dressed in all black and way above my height; he was perfect.

He tried his best to caress my chest, I couldn't decide if it was worth it; he tried to see how easy it would be to get to my soul.

He told me love songs that weren't really love songs and he encouraged my heart to grow cold.

It was pitch black; my valves were pumping pain.

Even after all of that, he couldn't remember my damn name.

My smile spread wider than legs downtown on a Friday night where someone's husband was being scandalous.

Gripping your seat won't prepare you for this ride, I simply don't think that you can handle this.

You see I loved him more than I could ever love me.

I am Porcelain

Guilt beat against my chest like rain, tell me how could this be?

How could darkness truly be the only light that I see?

22. <u>In Pain, I've Changed, & Now, I've Overcame</u>

It has been brought to my attention that all men are the same.

Whether it's your boyfriend or your father, all they leave you in is pain.

What's the possibility that they're at all who you can trust?

Seems as if lying and breaking promises is clearly a must.

I'm completely in disgust!

I tried to reverse the roles and flip the script, but it all came down in tragedy.

Reflecting on where I belong, I had to ask myself who's mad at me?

I'd say the woman in the mirror.

She's been trying to get my attention since day one, just begging for me to see her; but baffled and misled, I let the voices of a snake corrupt and occupy my head.

I am Porcelain

He manipulated me to his bed and released his venom into my veins, slowly sucking away the rest of my innocence in attempt for emotional damage in exchange.

So once again, I'm walking through the rain and I hope at the end of the day it's my dignity that I get to regain.

I was wanting gravity to keep me from going insane, or could it be that this shit just wasn't meant to maintain?

No picture perfect in a frame.

I felt the cells beginning to bake in my brain.

I needed to relax; mind racing, struggling, trying to figure out the facts.

I wanted to know who really had my back, and where the hell they were when I was picking up the slack?

I feel a cold winter coming on, tears falling while I'm still singing the same old song.

How many times will I reach for my phone and long for the vibrations of your voice?

I turned my back on you because you left me lingering in the wind with no choice.

More bruises and a broken heart to heal.

I am Porcelain

Close your eyes and simply imagine how a girl like me could possibly feel.

There's another dose of reality.

Lucifer backsliding and never hiding with the smoothest fatality.

It's okay, "I'm a big kid now," and I'll meet that woman in the mirror some way, somehow.

This is what it's like when it all boils down; the sun barely shines because you're never around.

My heart always waivers.

Please deliver me from the cliché "smile now and cry later."

23. *I Just Wish I Knew*

I just wish that I knew what happened to you.

I wish I knew why you had to go.

All of my crying along with my thoughts, just make me want to know.

I never would've wanted you to leave.

I didn't get a chance to say goodbye.

Looking back at all of our memories, I can't help but ask, why?

I never got a hug, any last words, or a chance to see your face.

I guess I shouldn't gripe for too long because people keep telling me that you're in a better place.

I miss you.

I never knew that your life was as crazy as I had heard.

I wish you would've talked to somebody or me because this isn't what you deserved.

I just wish that I knew what happened to you.

I wish I knew why you had to go.

I am Porcelain

All of my crying along with my thoughts, just make me want to know.

You were so fun to be around, and you could always make me laugh.

We had so many good times together, I just wish that I could get them back.

24. *Eternal Bruises*

My bruises are eternal because they'll never fade away.

Scarred for life is what I am, I face the music every day.

Sometimes I can hear my heart cry and question me of my hope.

I just rub my chest and shake my head because I'm at the very end of my rope.

I'm not sure what to say or exactly what to think.

All I ever wanted was for true love and affection but gone on forever more was lust and distant rejection.

Voices of my past mimic the beat of the drums dancing in my soul.

I can hear them beating loudly waiting for my story to be told.

Cruel intentions awaiting to unfold and release this

"someone" from within.

I asked the girl in the mirror, "is it you whom I should befriend and depend on?"

Confident in her silence, I knew that she would never do me wrong.

I am Porcelain

Picking up the phone I'm singing the sad, sad blues.

Dialing out a number, any number, just wanting to share my bad, bad news.

My bruises are eternal although I still believe in love.

Reflecting on my life, I wonder what my heart is even capable of.

No matter how much I hurt, I always dealt with the pain.

No matter how I saw the sun shining, I chose to walk through the rain.

It's a new season.

I'm changing pace.

No more tears.

I'm letting go of the girl who has haunted me for all these years.

25. *Crying Pains*

They've hurt me, they've judged me, and broke my heart inside.

They've yelled at me, tortured me, and hurt a portion of my pride.

They took away my joy and now I am forced to hide in my little black corner- where all girls cry.

All the happiness took away.

No love shown day after day.

Nothing but betrayal and heartache to match the stains upon my face.

Why can't they just let me be?

Why can't they depart all oceans from the seas and accept me for me?

There's no wall of separation, there's no sunshine, just darkness and anticipation.

There's a lonely soul just waiting, still trying to find her way home.

She is left to explore these tears all on her own.

I love love, but can love, love me?

I am Porcelain

I know that it never will so please just let me be free.

I just want to cry pain.

I just want to connect with the thoughts tucked away so deeply in the depths of my brain.

Don't you understand?

Falling in love with the enemy was never part of my plan.

26. *Church*

I am a sorry sinner because I am sorry that I sin, but

admitting my lack of obeying God's will is only half of where I shall begin.

I allow my lusts and temptations to consume my heart and mind.

I believed that the answer in fixing myself was through man and it was so hard to find, because I was wrong.

There is nothing more depressing than listening to sad songs, hurting.

Not realizing music can't heal me, I should be reading bible verses.

I look in the mirror every day and contemplate if my rebelliousness was worth it.

I'm far from scarred and so far from broken, or could it be that I'm so close that my lips won't reveal the unspoken?

You can find me choking in fetal position, trying to analyze what happened to my development.

Comfort zones are full blown, and I am way out of my element.

I am Porcelain

I said that I would love as if it were the only way for me to survive, but how exactly can I do that when I don't even feel alive?

When my heartbeat is suddenly silent, and I can't feel it from within my chest.

I tried to suffocate my skin in tight clothing, just to differentiate it from the rest.

I'm not this perfect picture, yet I'm not so bad.

I deal with pain the best way that I can, considering the life I've had.

My tainted souls, my damsels into stress, and my oh so withered lovers.

I come to you as your conscience and a side that you've yet to discover.

Peel yourselves from the floor and count your very many reasons to live.

I may not have the answers to everything, but this is all that I could give.

I never knew what it meant to truly heal until a church saved my life.

I am Porcelain

I was headed down a path of destruction, something about my soul just wasn't right.

I couldn't sleep at night, even when the angels whispered that everything would be okay.

I was so angry with God that I didn't even know what to say... about my broken heart, I just didn't understand.

I didn't know how to feel about my child and the tears that I cried but Jesus reminded me that our father had a plan.

He told me that temporary emotions were clouding the judgments that I had about leaving my life in his hands.

So, I decided to dance in reality and look hatred in the face.

I no longer feel dishonor or disgrace for my mistakes.

I've been asleep for so long but now, I'm wide awake.

27. It's Been Years

It's been years since I've saw you.

Why did you choose to walk away?

I really didn't know what to do.

I just cried day after day.

I remember staring at the phone just hoping that you would call.

Knowing that you were so wrong, I felt my heart fall.

I still sat and waited just hoping that it'd ring.

I guess that I waited for too long because I never heard a thing.

I wondered why us; how come you just didn't stay?

Why'd you come back, promise things, and make me feel this way?

I prayed, just hoping that you would come back to me.

I prayed that you'd see how much I made it, so that you could be whom you're supposed to be.

I feel caged.

I am Porcelain

You tossed burdens on my heart and now I'm forcefully full of rage.

I just wish that I could praise you but I'm afraid that I can't do that.

You walked out, left me, my twin, and my mother as a matter of fact.

It's been years since I've saw you and if only you knew- that everything you should've done; you really didn't have to do.

So, I'm asking you.

It's been a year since we've talked, why did that change?

We hid in closets to call you every day, but you still did the same damn thing!

You left and you never said goodbye!

There were always open chances, but you refused to give it a try.

My whole life I waited for the one man on my list to love- to love me back; but you didn't, you chose strangers over us.

Luckily, the father that I needed all along was always up above.

I am Porcelain

He let me know that I would be okay and to come to him when anything went wrong.

Moments came and I felt so nonexistent, he let me know that regardless, I DO belong.

You're just not who I thought you could be.

You came into our lives and then destroyed our family, mainly me.

Sinking into the seas of loneliness, I asked myself if we could ever coexist in this fistful of tears, but there's this irritation in my conscience reminding me… it's been years.

I am Porcelain

28. <u>Help Me</u>

Hey doc I'm having some problems and I don't know what to do.

I asked my friend for help and she directed me to you.

She said that you were honest and that you were discrete.

She said that you could do anything, there's nothing you can't defeat.

My heart has been aching and I feel beyond misused.

I thought my pain was over, but I guess I was confused.

These tears just keep on falling, why won't they go away?

I tried to channel my emotions; I just don't know what to say.

I feel a lump in my throat every time that I swallow.

Well doc can you fix me?

Will there be a better tomorrow?

Seems as if you're suffering from what we call broken heart syndrome and regret.

You'd love to move forward, but something's saying you haven't finished yet.

I am Porcelain

Your symptoms will vary within the lines of non-emotional flings and depression.

You'll try to counter this with mood swings as you justify your indiscretions.

The only medication I can provide is common sense and suggesting that you finally learn your lesson.

29. *Can You Save Me?*

I feel so hurt and lost; no way to go.

Both left and right, I feel as if I just don't know.

So many tears shed behind a love in its path.

I'm walking tall now, but why don't you feel my wrath?

I remain calm and try to analyze this terrible situation.

Fed up because no matter what, it's just so much temptation.

Trying to knock out the truth or what the future may hold.

Looking into the mirror I appear to be so bold.

Lovely, very glamorous, heart full of demands.

Nails on, everything going wrong, as I hold these decisions in my hands.

Dreams set on fire and a tongue left silent is how it feels to be in my world.

To be completely honest, this is also how it feels to have never been a little girl.

I never understood what it meant to just be a child and stay in my place.

I am Porcelain

So even in my adult years this is a stance I wish that I could take.

30. Bruises of A Lover's Fist

Do the bruises of a lover's fist leave you in pain?

Force you to hail in this thunderstorm due to the rain?

Or does it baffle you with love?

Treat you better than you've ever been treated, so that they're the one you're thinking of?

What about the touch?

So enduring and heartfelt that you just can't get enough.

Heart beating, skin bleeding, trying to figure out if this emotion is worth retrieving.

Or better yet believing.

I'm always falling to my knees.

Looking up to the good Lord, have mercy on me please.

I can hear him tell me that everything will be okay.

I just have to ask, what's going to take all the pain away?

He said, "My child, simply call me from beyond your dark skies."

With that being said he will always hear my cries.

A sweet bitterness uttered from a lonely goodbye.

31. *Self-Inflicted Wounds*

I was dead.

Completely frozen, so I thought, and I always felt that way.

Until I could taste the salty tears rolling down my face.

I always felt nonexistent.

Until my heart reminded me of pain.

I thought certain things would last a lifetime, but that would only be accurate if lifetime meant temporarily.

You see, I cropped your image into my memories.

I engraved all the times we had and favored the second that you befriended me.

Every night spent without you was a night not worth falling asleep. Even after you beat down on me, like rain on a Sunday morning.

I managed to crawl just to find my way back to you.

Imagine an imagination that didn't quite imagine anything. Hopeless, fearful, and overwhelmed with misunderstandings; that's why every time I hear the word poetry, my eyes grow wide and my heart beats as if true love found me.

I am Porcelain

Although, I'm not really sure if it did.

Certain subjects I run from, just as I do when I hear the word kids.

I never knew that a soul could cry until the very moment I acknowledged my loss.

But if I am ever blessed to carry another child again,

I'll name my baby Genesis, so that every time I look at him or her, I'll know that God granted me a new beginning.

Then again, maybe that's like my grandmother naming me innocent, because she hoped that I'd always be that way.

She never felt for one minute that her granddaughter would be gay and stray the long lines of lost causes; struggling to mend broken battles because I am very much broken.

Not meant to be fixed because I'm much better that way; torn to pieces.

I like to dig from within myself and analyze just where I went wrong.

But after pulling off every scab, I still can't quite determine exactly where I belong.

I am Porcelain

Somebody should have told me that being judged is equivalent to being dangled above everyone in the world, with a rope tightly knitted around your throat, promising to choke away all of who you are, while exposing everything you tried so hard not to become.

I have tried my best to accept that I won't be accepted, but how can I when I have to stare these people in the face quite often?

My storms are pouring down but instead of closing the curtains, I go out and allow the lightning to strike its truths within my flesh.

I dance with its anger boiling inside of me, you can feel the courage exploding from my chest.

I embrace my brokenness and I encourage my wounds to be exposed because they make me... exactly who I am.

32. Corruption

You tell me that you love me even though you don't.

My mind tells me to leave you but it's my heart that won't guide me away from the bruises that you imprinted on my skin.

Allow me to believe that I can be more than just a friend.

Your hands deliver stories to my body that were once faded away.

I hide from the reality of abuse as I face myself in the mirror every day.

"Please please please" I used to say and "Stop I'll do better."

Never understanding the entire time that you were whooping my ass; we weren't supposed to be together.

I thought that you would change.

I am Porcelain

I thought that after all of the women that you cheated on me with, that you would still remember my name, but you didn't.

I suddenly heard the warnings prior to this moment; I wish that I would've listened.

My mind was gone.

No matter how badly you treated me, I still felt that you could do no wrong.

I was naïve, I was corrupted.

33. My Existence

My soul is aching, and my heart is crying.

No more looking over my shoulder and no more lying.
I tried to swim but I went too deep.

The further I got; I couldn't feel me feet.

Emotionally paralyzed, I hit the bottom as I fainted.

I know you pulled me back up, but I am forever tainted.
Slowly sinking to my death

I'm under water, I can't breathe

Somebody please… help.

34. _I'll never clock out of life_

I try not to judge because I understand.

Tongue remaining silent as I'm clapping both of my hands.

I celebrate the madness… it's too much to maintain so why try to grasp it?

Plucking at my emotions as the pain is getting worse.

It suddenly becomes a sore; I can't believe how much it hurts.

Bittersweet memories fail to amuse me, analyzing this situation I find myself to be quite choosy.

Trying to come to terms with the way you used to abuse me.

I have a visual of pause, play, fast forward, and rewind, streaming through my thoughts effortlessly invading my mind.

I am Porcelain

I close my eyes sometimes I picture myself on the beach…dancing by the shore as the water and sand makes love to my feet.

I call it my imagination of hope… taking me away from reality and guiding me away from the rope, which so many people run to but see, I refuse to choke. Persuading myself not to let the negativity provoke cruel intentions, wrapped in a better saying that if someone talks you better listen.

Get the wax out of your ear.

Be bold and realize that all the ignorance you bring will never belong here.

Bottled up are the mistakes and regrets, I'm taking another chance because I haven't finished yet. Pay attention as I fade into the darkness.

I'm staying gone for a while so not even a match could spark this.

I am Porcelain

35. <u>Daddy's Little Girl's Confession</u>

I like movies where the father protects his daughter from anyone and everything, along with providing what she needs.

I love the relationships where a father will trade in his life just to ensure the existence of his seed.

I remember "Donuts for Dads" during school.

Who knew such a wonderful event could make me think so cruel?

The man I know to be my father isn't at all my father, he's a pedophile.

Nothing in this world about him could ever make me smile and far as my mother, I'd say she's in denial.

I cried harder than an infant after birth.

I travel the streets baffled because I don't know my own worth.

I am Porcelain

Oh, why did I deserve... to have daddy as my first.

As I write these words my fingers bleed because my veins are pumping sadness.

Crazy thing about it is nobody helped me through all of the madness.

I am a victim trapped in the body of a little girl.

Little girls shouldn't at all be victims because we haven't even developed a sense of right and wrong in the world.

Hurt, killed, damaged, or destroyed... I don't agree.

I was annihilated, simply reduced to nothing not understanding what this hardship means.

I was sexually degraded by my father until the age of 14, barely a teen.

I just wanted to him to pay, but nothing at all worked.

I confronted my mother and she didn't even believe me, imagine how bad I hurt.

I am Porcelain

I escaped the situation and even though I wanted out, I was a wreck that no one came to find me.

Discovering the darkness up close and personal was beyond blinding.

Who replaced morals, integrity, and parental values, in which he was supposed to possess?

Limited access to my emotions caused my soul not to rest.

Strapped in a double guarded vest; I should've been bullet proof.

These memories blow my mind like c4 I just wish that somebody knew.

Split personalities go back and forth inside of me yelling, screaming, kicking and crying.

Every time you touched me, I felt as if I were dying.

"I thought that I was put here for you to love... not so you could use me!

I am Porcelain

Daddy you were supposed to protect me, not molest me, upset me and abuse me.

You cruised my adolescent skin with your demented intentions and perverse ways.

I secretly wished those hands made their to my neck and killed me one day.

Daddy's little girl was nothing I thought it should've been.

I desired a life of tea parties, dressing up, and playing pretend.

A day where you could meet my friends and we'd mend tall tales, pizza, and ghosts.

My mind was corrupted therefore my childhood was a hoax.

Your vision of playing pretend was incorporated by sadistic beliefs that I was more than just a daughter to you.

Did you look in the mirror one day and say "Tonight I'll play the fool"

I am Porcelain

I'll drool like the dog I am and haunt her for the rest of her life.

Coming out of my mother's womb I wasn't prepared for such strife.

All our lives we exist to create beautiful memories so that when we die, we can have something to dream about.

I don't get to dream anymore.

How could you do this to me?

What could I have done?

You were battling between heaven and hell, so I guess the devil won."

I am Porcelain

36. *Jasmine Mans*

I never put lip gloss on my vagina, but I admit that it was very close to heart.

I was longing for a kiss of love hoping never to fall apart.

So, what if I told you that the "little girl" was me?

What if I said that I was only twelve years old and that I thought that it was okay because I had big feet?

I try to distance myself from what I feel can't be forgiven.

I am slowly going to continue now that I have your full attention.

See tampons were always my favorite, but I let my thoughts of temptation and rebelliousness consume me, so I crashed… into a ditch.

Everywhere I turned I thought only a penis could fix.

My candles remained lit, but I was so broken.

I am Porcelain

Deception lying next to me as I remained soft spoken.

I used eyeliner to outline the darkness that I was exposed to and it never failed.

The lines blended in with the pitch-black memories of guilt and a pinch of hell.

I never had to stuff my bra because in my mind, a heart didn't exist, therefore, I didn't feel alive.

It cracked right along with that fucking glass slipper, because only the men could hear me cry.

I was shouting for acknowledgment, but no one knew that I was there.

So, I did whatever I felt could ease the pain, as I embraced more than I could bear.

I felt like a child in a classroom, jumping up and down with my hand rose, yelling "me, me, me," hoping the teacher would take out the time to listen, and finally encourage me to speak.

I am Porcelain

All my life was I was worried about the bruises of a lover's fist and how it would affect my existence.

I tried to stay focused, I promise, but man was that devil persistent.

"Do this," "Do that," and "Do it some more," he would say from the side of my neck.

So, I would freely listen replying "Awww shit what the heck… what's the worst that could happen?"

Before I knew it, I looked back and my childhood was kidnapped; so, I respond to your poem asking who do I go after?

Is it too late to save this body that's drowned in sin?

Sometimes I choke in my sleep due to the inability to swim… far away.

I didn't have to distract anybody from what they never saw in the first place.

I am Porcelain

Rape was a form of love for me until I began to bleed somewhere unusual.

You're right, I didn't know how to love myself properly because my soul was on its way to my funeral.

Not only did I shed tears the first time, I shed them every time!

Wondering when I would play with the dolls that I had, instead of myself, or reach out to the other side of me that I know needed help because…

I miss my cartoons, cotton candy, and the mental protection from the world.

I am twenty-one years old now and I still feel like that little girl!

Even after I pulled my pants up, I still felt the wind whopping my ass.

Maybe I should've let my father save me like you said… I just want my childhood back.

I am Porcelain

If you don't put alcohol on your scars, then you will never know what it means to burn.

I look deeply into my past and I know that there were many lessons learned, but how do I cast out the ghost of a virgin girl?

How do I tell her that it's all over and that there is no changing the world, even if you try?

How do I stare into the mirror and wave to her my final goodbye, although I know that I'll be seeing her again?

Is it possible to believe that you can replace my Crayola fingers with strips of white-out to lay over my mistakes?

Is there any hope of calming the emotions that shake within me harder than any seizure or earthquake?

After living in denial for so long I'm wide awake.

You helped me see that being a little girl isn't easy.

My heart is bleeding hatred because I just want to tell her sorry, but I don't think that she'll believe me.

I am Porcelain

Here I walk down the trail of lost lives, shaking the hands of the ones that dance alone, but still stand within the bodies of missing persons.

Suddenly it's a CSI investigation trying to figure out who's really hurting.

How do I mark the spot, criminal, or perpetrator?

Who should I tell you finger-fucked my childhood out of me?

Because I want to see you jump at victory after the thumb wrestling match for it back is finished?

It's been ten years since the betrayal and my conscience has yet to be replenished.

Instead, I confront my innocence that was quickly diminished.

Listening to your poem led me to believe that you ache for the children that don't have anyone to ache for them in

I am Porcelain

return, because their skies always dot the surfaces black, red, and blue.

Listening to your poem brings me to a conclusion that I, I love you too.

So, for every raindrop that caresses my pillow I'll always think of you.

I'll think of the way that I felt after hearing the truth; which is that I was getting fucked harder than a man on death row, paying for a crime that he didn't commit, and the sad thing is I didn't even know.

So, no matter how I try to push through my past I will never forget that my mind was in a land beyond bewilderment, and now it's running faster than a thug from a crime scene.

Growing up I never realized what I would be saying now or what the depth of pain really means.

So, here is my response and my story because through it all, I am still standing therefore God has the glory, and He always will.

"Just because your feet fit perfectly into your mother's shoes that that does not make you a woman... little girl"

I am Porcelain

This is my acknowledgment that you're right and I agree.

This is not just a poem… this is me.

Inspired as a response to my favorite poet, Jasmine Mans.

37. Flawless Perceptions

I was more than uneasy, believe me; I had been infected.

This disease compelled my entire body, no way could I reject it.

I wondered why medication couldn't control this situation.

Inflated with the truth and taunted with anticipation.

Content, that not everyone can possess such a challenge to be genuine.

Being accepted was a battle with the skin that I was forced to live in.

You wonder what it is and why am I not sad?

I take pain for fun; motionless to the betrayal I've had.

Men don't get wet, they get hard!

So, trade the pussy in and let's see if you can match my scars.

I am Porcelain

The Doctor told me that this fatal discovery and I will always be together.

Chances are I'll do more than die with it, we'll mingle inseparably forever.

I suffer from an illness that is described as "being real."

It can spread like a wildfire, having no physical, emotional, or sexual appeal.

Those who don't have it flee from its existence or reality.

Tragedy of reflections embodied from their past, manipulate their integrity causing their souls not to last.

Trapped in a maze, ignorant as to what's going on.

I'm happy to be infected, just know you'll never do me wrong.

I'm strong;

I fight for respect, wisdom and success.

So next time you read my shit, go ahead and admit I'm the best.

38. I Control You

He didn't break my heart; he broke my soul.

He ripped it into two and had the nerve to call me cold.

As I watched his fear unfold, I realized that there was some truth that needed to be told.

I held his only chance at life in my own very hands, but this wasn't nearly enough for me.

I wanted him to shrivel at my feet along with my plans.

I wanted him to love me the way that he should've in the first place.

A man will only do what allow him to do; no more dwelling on childish mistakes.

I hold the power... henceforth, I control you.

I am Porcelain

39. <u>*Gay Pride*</u>

In this world, there are only so many things that you can pay for, but money can't buy you everything.

You can't pay somebody to love you.
You can't pay somebody to care.

I love the smell of sweet perfume; the kind that is transferred from me hugging my loved one closely.

I love kissing her and watching her eyes roll to the back of her head, when I assist her in reaching her climax.

I love women.

I love their curves and their smiles.

I love making them feel acknowledged and wanted.

I love what some of the people in this world are taunting me and hating me for loving.

So, who am I supposed to love? Huh?

I am Porcelain

Who's supposed to love me back?

There are so many people that share the same desires as me.

I believe that there is someone for everyone whether you are light, dark, fat, skinny, tall, short, ugly, or gay.

But for some being gay isn't an option… it's a problem, although my sexual orientation has nothing to do with them.

You love who you love, and I love who I love… even harder.

But what's love got to do with it, if you have people judging you for connecting and sharing the most intimate moments together?

Do we think as a human race that hating will make our opinions sound any better?

I love her and I want to touch her because her body is mine.

I am Porcelain

I sleep with her and I want to be with her because she was a part of my first time.

It's okay to be a sinner, as long as you're not gay?

I wake up every morning realizing that I love being this way.

If I were a male, it would be the twitch in my walk and the high pitch in my voice.

Whatever I choose to do in my bedroom is beyond my choice, but to the world, me and those of whom share the same passions aren't accepted?

What about fornicators, adulterers, liars, and thieves?

Aren't they too rejected?

There are marriages that condone adultery and tie into things that you wouldn't believe.

I am Porcelain

Yet certain organizations, businesses, and individuals want to focus their judgments on me.

Don't you have something more to be worried about?

This world as a whole is failing, but you're more concerned with where I'm putting my mouth?

The words that travel from your lips are nothing but ignorant and hypocritical.

The fact that you view your sins more differently than mine is just pitiful.

But I'm not here to make you love me, I just want you to see who I am on the inside because you preach that "God don't like ugly."

Everyone wants to shout about their rights but they're the ones doing the most wrong.

Tell me, do you have to watch your back more than often as you trail the sidewalks on your way home?

Should I control, limit, or change my sexuality because it doesn't meet your standards or expectations?

The fuck I look like?

I am Porcelain

Last time I checked I don't owe you an explanation.

The same ones yelling that hell has my name on it will be meeting Satan long before I do.

Put it all out there on the table and share what point you THINK you have to prove.

I know that your brain has tainted you into believing that your simple mindedness doesn't make you look stupid or as a fraud.

I know before you became Christian or whatever you are, you didn't always know God, or carry his words upon your heart.

You fail to realize that all the time you waste bashing my existence you'll be the one falling apart.

For a human connection alone, there is no love that can compare to the ways in which we share what we refuse not to hide.

Ordinary couples battle within bedrooms to keep secrets but we, we embrace our gay pride.

I am Porcelain

She comforts me in my weakest moments, stares deeply into my eyes and never lies about how maintaining such a love can be fatal.

Some hold hands, but it's my heart that she cradles, gently promising not to squeeze the only fight I have left in my soul.

I tell her that we will prevail, although this world is so cold.

We will have to walk the trails of history to obtain our rights just as many have done before.

Women, African Americans, Biracial Lovers and so many more.

I adore the possibility that one day I can love freely.

You may think that I'm the scum of the earth, but there are women who will love me because I am beautiful.

You will never tear me down.

Down like when her head is in between my legs, as they are wrapped around her neck, clenching every bit of the sensation that she is sharing through the vibrations of her tongue.

iBleedPoetry

I am Porcelain

Slowly switching positions, letting go of the swords that's been swung- to cut the only hopes of meeting our only one.

You may think that when she's eating my pussy that that's all that she's doing, but when she's down there she eats away my insecurities and my thoughts of being ashamed, so when I cum it's considered to be rain... drops.

Lifting up my leg as she sips my tears, I don't want her to stop because she encourages my confidence.

I remember when my family found out that I was rooting for the same gender as myself.

I thought that they would disown me, along with suggesting my need for help, but after the shock wore off, I was surrounded with support.

So why do you feel you have to belittle me and pass judgments as if you are going to be the one banging the gavel in court?

I sing to those that are just like me because I know what they are feeling.

I am Porcelain

For us to go through such a dramatic change, how do you know this isn't our way of healing?

Molestation, rape, or just growing up under the influences and persuasions that this world has to offer, I sing.

I still sing because my heart is so heavy.

The reflection staring back at me in the mirror is constantly convincing me to hold it steady, but I still sing.

I still sing because my heart is so heavy.

The reflection staring back at me in the mirror is constantly convincing me to hold it steady, but I still sang and the words that made their way back to me were so amazing.

In the midst of it all I kept hearing "colors."

So, I stopped singing like the birds that echo tunes of a lost love, and I listened to this misty appearance that broke me down to my knees.

Tears rolling down my cheeks faster than any river I listened.

Because the words that made their way back to me were so sweet, so incomparable, so amazing.

I am Porcelain

This woman from within my reflection kept going on and on, so I listened, and I heard all that I needed to know.

She gave me confidence that overwhelmed my insecurities.

So, I listened and when I finally heard her clearly, I sang too.

I sang because the heaviness that weighed tons on my heart took pride in my joy.

I lay in my bed and I face the public with these words because they are so sweet, so incomparable, so amazing.

She looks into my eyes every second of the day and she whispers to me.

She whispers to me.

"I see your true colors shining through. I see your true colors and that's why I love you. So, don't be afraid to let them show, your true colors, true colors are beautiful like a rainbow."

These words are so incomparable, so sweet, so amazing.

The song quoted is Cyndi Lauper's "True Colors," I do not own copyrights to this music.

40. *A Flow of Confusion*

Drowned with his ability to basically let me breathe.

I'm troubled with no help, dangerously falling to my knees.

Faces and secrets always hiding in the dark.

He loves me or could it be… he loves me not?
It's exactly what I thought.

Going, going, going out of control.

I got myself in, I can get myself out; below and behold.
Nature speaks in a voice so sweet; it's strange.

I try obligating myself with too much to maintain.

I possess this special sensation; you can see it in my veins.

A swarm of lies and deceit.

I am Porcelain

Moving fast or just thinking slow; red light, yellow light, somebody tell me when to go.

I am Porcelain

41. <u>A Book & Its Cover</u>

I always wondered if you could ever hear me cry.

Soul left behind somewhere floating in the sky.

Heart ready to die and mind, fainted.

Appearance on the outside almost feels as though I've been painted.

But I'm not just some pretty picture, there is so much more to see.

Everything that really matters is deep inside of me.
You've all taken me for granted and I'm not sure why.

Yet I still have the courage to fasten my seat belt to give love another try.

Wind blowing in my face, caressing my hair.

I turned around to look because it seemed like you were there.

I am Porcelain

You left me with the naked truth and exposed me to your lies.

All of the pain that I have is your fault, and yet you still can't tell me why.

42. *I Quit*

Does the encounter of one's lips to yours compare to the enclosure of their affection?

Does the pressure of anonymous emotions fulfill your wish for your protection?

Can you ever place a medal or reward the way that he makes you feel?

Has he ever opposed reality just by being real?

I question all statements and judge all answers due to my theory.

With so much corruption to display, you still cannot hear me!

For a second chance is ruined and will never take place.

You're rotten, spoiled, and full of disgrace.

I refuse to put up with who you are, and I won't allow it anymore… this is it.

I am Porcelain

I've fought harder than I've ever had to… and now… it's over, I quit.

43. Breaking Away

Drowned in his authority, I need to be set free.

Strangled with emotion is the breath of my ability.

Blind as the mastermind opens one path for me to seek.

Traveling back to reality, I have reached my final peek.

Steady beating into my heart is the fantasy of this other world.

Splitting it into two dimensions, I see I'm no ordinary girl.

Imagine tasting hatred with thoughts of letting go.

I've taken bullets to my head and it all came from one blow.

Shooting lyrics from my arrow, hoping they hit their only target of pain.

I'm mentally burning in this fire.

Pinpointing myself with no further desire.

Hurting is an emotion not a choice.

So, the moment that you endure the pain, -

say something because it could be your final voice.

44. The Disappearance

She's gone forever.

She's never coming back.

As we gather here today, we hope that wherever she is, she's okay.

We have to fight for the hope and possibilities of a better tomorrow.

Drain every sign of negativity and accept the sorrow.

A building of tears with fears that seem to be elastic.

They bounce back reminding you of your tragedies and smother you like plastic.

What happened to all of the smiles and innocent laughter that accompanied the fun?

Where did she go the last day that we saw her after lying under the sun?

Vanished.

I am Porcelain

Who knew she would really disappear?

No love and no attention joined by the silent tears.
Minions of Satan are steady calling her name.
Trying to plant this bomb in many areas of her brain.
Will she ever return?

How much will she experience before she actually learns?
I always wonder if I will ever see her again.

Her smile shined the brightest; she was my only friend.

Looking out of my window and into the mirror I know,
she's gone forever…

I am Porcelain

45. *Unpredictable*

We live in a time where your ex-boyfriends could someday be lovers.

A day where he can tell you that he saw something within his soul that you'd never see.

A moment where they'd only share the betrayal of your heartache and stomach the judgment of this world.

I could be dreaming, but I really doubt that I am because I would spend nights listening to him cry his name while he's sleeping.

He'd mistake our love making for theirs, imagine my face while weeping.

I was creeping behind dresser drawers just to hear their conversations on the phone.

I should be highest paid actress, because I would have to play happy when he'd tell me that he was leaving home... to go to work.

I am Porcelain

He didn't have a damn job, imagine how bad I hurt.

I'd slit my wrist just to see the tears that I would bleed.

I was waiting for him to tell me that I was all he'd ever need.

Needless to say, he never did.

I sometimes often wonder when they hold each other if either one of them see my face or if when they make love, do they remember the way that I taste?

I mean how could HE take MY place?

I'm supposed to be remembered.

I am not supposed to be the girl faded away into September...

Blue skies while the angels cry waiting for November.

I am Porcelain

46. <u>We're the Same</u>

If I stared into your soul, I wonder what I would see.

Would I witness a barrier breaking deep inside of me?

Gazing at the sky it seems to remind me of your eyes and the sun when it's shinning, I envision your smile.

So, if only for a little while, illuminate my path of destruction.

Provide a mask and let me find my way to corruption, because I long to be broken.

I wish to be remembered.

I am hoping for better days even after November.

Could you kiss me for the sake of our history?

Can you love my heart because you soulfully love me?

Will you eat my pussy until my legs shake and give me your all until after my back breaks?

I never believed that there's a thin line between love and hate, until now.

I am Porcelain

So, show me how to love until I know to.

Inject me with that drug, enhance my intellect with the meaning of us.

I can't count the missing pieces to this puzzle but give me a reason to try to put them together anyway.

Tell me that even though my dreams are shattered I'll still be okay.

I can still fly.
I can still soar dangerously if I just try.

Embrace my positivity and cradle it as if it were the child I were supposed to have.

Look into my heart and convince me that I'm not that bad.

I'm just... like... you.

47. _Forbidden Love_

Trapped in the pits of lust, I found you in my emotions.

You took me away like poison or some hypnotic love potion.
I suddenly aspired to become your truest devotion.

Taken by surprise, I never thought that I would see a strand of love in your eyes.

You brought sunshine through the midst of my constant grey skies.

Who was I to think that these feelings could ever hide? They were so wrong.

I can't continue to fall for you, but I just know that I am not alone.

Possibilities of vulnerability are obvious but aren't I always?

I am Porcelain

Aren't I always lost in destruction longing for a different source of heart ache?

But this is a chance I'm willing to take.

I feel as though I'm supposed to give your heart a break.

A break from typical dates and temporary forms of mistakes.

I didn't believe that I could fall and never care to get back up again.

I'm confused because lots of people say that I should only feel this way for men.

Therefore, my soul aches for answers and thoughts of your presence spread through my brain like cancer.

I hold steady under the moonlight hoping to be your one and only dancer.

Undress my insecurities and help me expose them for what they truly are.

I am Porcelain

I've searched the skies and I feel as though I've found my lucky star.

Regardless of our positions, shine brighter than any diamond or pearl.

I'm aware that it hasn't been long, but you've made me happier than I've ever been in this world.

I know that I may be lost but can we be lost together? Can we connect missing pieces of our souls even if it doesn't last forever?

It would illuminate my life if only for one night or just a little while.

I guess I'm head over heels because you always give me a reason to smile.

I am Porcelain

48. *Love Like This*

One thousand hugs. One million kisses. So many dreams.

So many wishes.

Out of every guy I've ever met. You're the one I won't forget.

God chose you for me from all the rest.

He knew deep down inside that we would connect.

My heart was full of faith, all that I dreamed came true. There is no longer a battle or barrier; it's simply just me and you.

My heart is similar to a pot of gold.

It's so hard to get and so hard to hold.

Visions of us together in Heaven is where the skies are always blue.

I am Porcelain

But just in case you don't make it, I'll leave Heaven just to be with you.

49. _Her_

Her lips feel like poetry to me and her eyes see me in a light that I never knew existed.

Her hands give me the chills and I drown in her voice.

I escape my worries through her presence because my heart leaves me no choice.

So quickly I love her and so quickly I am falling.

Her words pierce my soul like bullets because her mind is steady calling... my name.

She makes all the difference when I analyze the pain.

It doesn't rain anymore... the sun is always shinning down on me and it seems elementary, but if this happiness is only temporarily, I'd still cherish the hugs, the time, and the kisses.

I'd pray that there was something more for me to experience... but it'd still be her that I'd be missing.

I see nothing but a beautiful garden when I think about her, my emotions hold so much power.

I am Porcelain

I just want to walk through the dirt barefoot just to embrace the smell of every flower.

I am Porcelain

50. *Want Me*

When she talks to you, I wonder if her vagina throbs to the sound of your voice, I would know because my pussy jumps every time you call.

I wonder if her ears wait to hear you laugh or if you even matter at all.

I just KNOW that you do…

This bitch drives me crazy because my intuition tells me she would die just to have you.

I am a volcano. I erupt every time I hear her name, but it's something you'll never understand so it's a matter that you have failed to change.

The memory of you both stomp my presence like feet on a rug, but would you believe me if I said I'm in love?

I want you more than a little girl wants a pony at the age of five.

You caress my heart with your existence because you make me feel so alive.

I am Porcelain

I don't know why the disagreements; I don't know why the pain.

I try to duck and go for cover when there's a slight chance of rain.

I never think about anything else; I just want to have you in my arms.

I want to feel your body against mine, I simply just wanted to belong.

You tied into my mind and fed happiness to my soul.

Ignited with tears invited, I felt this heartbeat getting old.

Don't you like to hear it anymore?

Am I no longer the girl that you wish to adore?

I try to persuade you to trust that I love you, to trust that I care.

I am Porcelain

I try to convince you that no matter what I'll always be right there, lying next to you, so that you can wake up to me a thousand times.

I'll get mad at you for many things but reality sinks in that we'll be fine.

I understand your previous frustrations and I'm aware of your misconceptions, but the aches in my heart persuade me to believe that our linking up is a blessing.

My darling you possessed me with a light of acceptance and in all actuality, I thought that I provided you with that same light.

The only thing that matters is that I get to hold you every night.

Baby I want you to share a passion with me greater than the word itself.

I want you to want me and nobody else, but even if you say you do then provide more than a mouthpiece; give me physical.

I'm used to show and tell, so if you don't know that by now then you don't know me very well.

I am Porcelain

I want you to want me.

I want you to need me.

I want you to have me and hold me; give me all of who you claim to be.

Lay me down and relax my insecurities.

Listen to me make those sounds, -

make me cum.

Use your senses and embrace the fact that I just may be your only one.

51. Sex w/ You

Her tongue spoke to me in a language that I thought I never knew.

I couldn't really hold a sentence until she was completely through.

Her fingers found happiness within me as I started to flow.
She went places that I thought no one could ever go.

My ooooh's and ahhh's and moaning her name sent me into orgasms; thought I was going insane, but I wanted the pain.
I wanted her to dig inside of me as if she had found treasure.

I felt so guilty because of how much I enjoyed this pleasure.
I laid there shaking as I let her mouth read my vagina a love letter.

I allowed her to bury herself within my walls.

The further I moved back the more she would crawl- like a lion on the hunt after its prey.

I am Porcelain

She never knows how her making me cum gets me through the day, so I wanted her to constantly make me feel this way. Head tilted back as she watches the expressions on my face. She whispers sweet nothings into my ear, her voice gives me the shakes.

With this girl, I've felt things I've never felt.

I've had chills down my spine and butterflies in my stomach.

I was really hesitant at first but ohhh baby I want this... day and night.

I want her to taste me until her saliva becomes my juices, and I won't let her stop until I smell myself when I kiss her. Even after the amount of time gone by, I still cannot resist her.

I love the way she stares into my eyes and when she looks away.

I lay her on her back.

I promise I will surprise you, just do me a favor and relax.

Let me give you all this energy that my tongue will never get back.

I am Porcelain

Please get on top of me, climb me like a mountain.

Let me touch you here and kiss you there, sip you like a fountain.

Ride me like a horse and as you get closer to your climax, I will be waiting for your voice to break while asking if I came too.

I will grip your thighs and wait for the rain to run; I now have one more moment to bask in.

You have given me the best sexual experience that even a nympho could ever imagine.

52. My Dove

Why does the tree sing a better tune than the bird?

How come there's a lot to be said but still I hear no words?

Why does the mouth of the beholder keep all darkness, truth, and pain behind?

Take away what's mine and leave me to resign position.

I try to whisper affection, but the bird never listens.

So, I sit in the tree and wait for the bird to come to the branch and he does.

I always figured the bird was pushing me away, but he never really was.

He just flew to a destination beyond my path and a surprise to my discovery and mind.

Through the process of this branch breaking, things began to unwind.

I am Porcelain

Even the flowers around the tree were starting to question the bird and why he was so quiet.

When the bird decided to sing, all he ever did was deny it.

Why? Because the bird had a special tune playing in his heart.

He didn't want it to affect someone else.

He just wanted to live the tune all for himself...

But the tree tried to whisper more affection at a certain point.

The bird unknowingly broke all joints and hurt tree, but it built up and shaped into me.

The branches are parts of my heart and the bird is my one true love that's holding back.

What can I say after all these emotions are stacked?

Besides he's broken me down cry after cry... he won't express himself and I don't know why.

iBleedPoetry

I am Porcelain

So, I grow my branches longer and allow the sunshine to make it better.

So that when the bird comes back, he'll know we'll always be together.

In that special spot where all flowers grow and people fall in love, the bird is my branch and my special white dove.

53. <u>*Confrontations w/ the Dove*</u>

I'm tired of being hurt and emotionally abused.

I'm sick of being fed up and always being misused.

If I could love and receive love in return.

I would sit back and relax because I know a lesson has been learned.

That lesson would be appreciation, caring, and recognition.

Truth is I'm tired of talking to the bird that never listens.

When will my flowers bloom?

When my flowers bloom, the sun is my smile.

The rain is for when I cry every once in a while.

The petals on my flower are crushed without a care.

I don't want love given to me if it was never there.

When my flowers bloom, it indicates that I'm proud.

I am Porcelain

This feeling is something remarkable because for once my head isn't in the clouds.

When my flowers bloom my heart does too.

Guess you could say that's the moment when you know that I love you.

Once my flowers bloom, I'll know if down your path is where I'm willing to go.

So, remember my flowers and watch them grow, day by day.

The trick to knowing when they'll bloom is once you feel the same way.

54. _Dreaming of Your Kiss_

As the wind blows, I can hear you erotically whispering my name.

Making love to my emotions, your lips ease all the pain.

Within every inch of rain, the sun begins to shine.

I'm baffled by this chemistry; your heart beats the same time as mine.

As I endure this roller coaster of imagination, I see your face.

Sharing the sweetest kiss, there is no better taste.

55. *Those Eyes*

I stand in the wind just to let my hair blow.

Something screaming at my soul as I tell myself not to let go.

I knew that it was him although he didn't say.

He clung to me softly in that warm and gentle way.

Don't listen to the corruption of his mind.

The eyes of a liar never leaves a soul behind.

56. Love

Gentle hugs.

Soft kisses.

All I ask for is forgiveness.

All of the times that I wasn't there, doesn't mean that I did not care.

Believe in me now because I'm so for real.

No one would know the way that I feel.

Take my hand and follow me.

If you don't know, then you'll be led to see.

Please understand me at this time.

If I could, I would rewind.

I am Porcelain

Rewind those times I let you down.

Made you upset because I wasn't around.

I just want to love you.

57. *Love is*

Love is something found and never planned.

It's something treasured but you can never understand.

Love is how you feel ...

It's not fake or made up... love is real.

Truth is, I never had a broken heart.

I had a broken mind for allowing me to believe that I did.

58. *Love Affair*

Sacred touches, secret kisses, and foul corruptions of my heart.

Nothing but hiding, left alone defying something that you wanted to start.

There's a part of me that knows you don't cherish what I sacrificed.

All of the creeping around that we did, I wanted to be your wife.

I was nothing more than your mistress.

Late nights were all I had… guess no mind games could fix this.

Stalking your every move wondering when you were leaving her.

I look better, I cater to your needs, and I am the woman in which you deserve.

I am Porcelain

Sinking into the heartache of our existence; recognizing my only place.

She has the ring and I don't… boy did I made a huge mistake.

Office flings that seemed like a beautiful thing, bearing the lusts of true emotions.

You always got exactly what you wanted while I was the one left hoping.

Never having the say of when we get to meet.

No open romances, we had it to keep it discrete.

I was forced to accept the rank of being number two.

I could have had anyone I wanted, but truth is… I was in love with you.

The sex was simply amazing but aside from that I thought you'd care.

I am Porcelain

Naïve from what my heart forced me to believe… I was just your love affair.

I am Porcelain

59. <u>Marry Me</u>

It was just like yesterday and you were holding me into your arms.

Squeezing me tightly saying nothing would ever go wrong.

You said to me that you loved me and that these things would never change.

I remember because you knelt down on one knee and asked to change my last name.

I am Porcelain

60. <u>*Making Love*</u>

I can feel him touching my face as it appears, he's not touching me at all.

But with words and just one kiss, he simply makes my heart fall.

Deep into my lower body, making me weak.

I lose all balance because he knocks me off my feet.

Perpetrating a withered lover, I quickly become sad.

Pregnant with opportunity, I'm lifted to this place that's not so bad.

Romeo and Juliet were very happy together but ended up alone.

Due to differences that were juvenile or rather misunderstood.

I was slowly taking faster paces within every chance that I could.

I am Porcelain

Flowers in my garden confused on how to pick.

I'm blushing harder than I ever have, hoping that he doesn't quit.

Feathers imitating the actions of your tongue, I quiver when you utter my name.

Inhaling the smell of cologne, I pray this experience will never change.

61. *Happy Valentine's Day*

Today I hope that you're happy because I want you to be.

My joy is when we are laughing, there's still some sadness inside of me.

But even though we have our ups and downs, we finally know our love is found.

Baby I'm on my way, Happy Valentine's Day.

My love goes out there for you because I know that it's true.

It just stays in one place to help recover the love we make.

And even though we have our ups and downs, we finally know our love is found.

Baby I'm on my way, Happy Valentine's Day.

I am Porcelain

I am Porcelain; The

Naked Truth

Crown Adjusted.

iBleedPoetry

Fatherless Child; A Change Gone Come

As I mentioned, I grew up without my father. I honestly never thought that he'd return but, in the year of 2010, he came back into my life and never left. He became persistent in wanting to spend time with myself and all of his other children, but because I had gotten used to him not being there, his presence wasn't a priority to me. I also carried spitefulness in my heart for my younger siblings, because who were they to have deserved my father at his best? I longed to be a *Daddy's Girl* while growing up. It took a lot of time for me to look at his other children and not feel negatively towards them, but it happened, and I have grown to understand that although I missed out, it doesn't change his love for me, and it shouldn't alter his love for them.

My father gave me several reasons to hate him, but he spent years repairing what he had broken. He modeled something for me that I had only witnessed on television; a man.

I am Porcelain

He began by explaining the way that things happened back then, and as much as I called bullshit before, it's different, because now, I comprehend what it means to be young and to make mistakes. I was able to forgive him because he displayed that my forgiveness was important to him.

My twin loved him and forgave him with no problem, but me- I was the angry sister; as I told you, I have trouble letting go of things. My nose would flare at the sight of him, I was just like my mother. Her anger for him was embedded in me, until I realized that I DID in fact want to be his daughter; I had all along.

I was surprised to learn that my father was fun, hilarious, and cool. He made up for moments that he missed throughout my childhood by being there for every important endeavor in my adulthood.

My father has been present for every birthday, every book signing, and every spoken word performance that I've had. He was there for me when my mother passed away; he held me together.

I am Porcelain

I have not been very active in his life, due to insecurities and battles of my own, but I am going to start with him as he did with me; communicating and showing up.

I am sorry for those of you whom still lack a relationship with your fathers, because I know that pain all too well. I wanted to share this in the hopes that I give you a little faith in recovering the traumas of your childhood. If you don't get to have your own father back, I pray to GOD that you receive a father figure, but you must be open to accepting the love and guidance, even if you'd rather it be from your own dad.

It is important for us to have a man that we look up to, so that we will remember how we should be treated and how we should be loved. It feels good to have my father around because I truly do feel protected. I feel whole again.

I wish you well.

I am Porcelain

Some Words for

You . . .

It's apparent that I've changed over the course of the years.

I want to say that it's been for the better, but honestly, I am still currently trying to figure that out; as I'm sure a lot of you are.

What I want to share are the new to you and old to me poems; all painfully orchestrated after the first release of The Naked Truth.

Farewell, *for now*.

I am Porcelain

62. *Better*

I used to whisper love songs to the devil, simply hoping that I could change him.

Used to ignore his ill intents, I was longing to rename him.

I'm just wondering...

At what age do I experience my mid-life crisis?

I'll name myself Cardi Chanel, wear clothes that are too small, and pretend that I don't have to do what is righteous.

I'll daydream the life that I've always wanted; it'll be like art to my white walls.

I won't get a motorcycle, no never a motorcycle, because I'm far too afraid to fall.

Little did I know, I had already fallen.

So, to the woman who damn near cries when someone asks her "how are you?" because in the back of her mind she's wondering if you really want to know, I hear your truth.

I feel your pain.

But you are far more than your struggle and you are being prepared for a change.

I am Porcelain

Don't doubt this season.

We get so caught up in the logistics of life, that we always feel that we need a reason from GOD, but we don't.

We know better.

So, tell them.

And by them, I mean the devil, I mean your opposers, I mean the worst versions of yourselves.

Tell them.

I bet you didn't think that I knew better than to allow you to defile my potential.

To challenge my authority.

To mangle my character.

I bet you didn't think.

They say that you can't reclaim your virginity.

Chyle please!

My jewel was imported from Jesus himself.

No, I will NOT just GIVE it to you.

I bet you didn't know.

I am Porcelain

I bet you didn't know that I knew better.

Your hostility does not move me, I am solid.

You see diamonds, diamonds get dirty too.

We may have fallen to the ground, attracted dust and dirt but we are still diamonds.

We often find strength to be present for others when we can't even show up for ourselves.

WE are still diamonds.

I know.

I know that drama and mess get so bad that you wonder if GOD is telling your business too.

But that is when you learn how powerful and humbling your silence is.

For whomever has forsaken you shall soon be forgotten.

So, when they ask, tell em yo money good and life is great!

And if you feel that you're lying when you say this, then make that lie your truth!

Tell them.

Tell em that you reciprocate positivity, ONLY.

I am Porcelain

Tell them that you don't settle for complacency, even if that means being lonely.

Tell them!

Tell them that you have no room for minds that are not compatible.

For tongues that only represent gossip!

For men that only love you when it's convenient for them!

For shots covered in compliments!

For shade that's been falsified to be sunshine!

For synthetic support!

Watered down apologies and pain on purpose!

Tell them!

Tell them that you know better.

Because I bet, they don't THINK... that you do!

63. *Fire in the Sky*

You were a fire from the sun to me.

Streaming effortlessly as if you were the only bird in the sky.

The devil himself could clip your wings, and somehow, you'd still be able to fly.

You found me in fetal position, I was laying in the grass.

My eyes were completely closed, yet I still couldn't look pass you.

I can normally see when someone is coming, or at least when they are close.

But you caught me totally off guard; our love was bonded tighter than rope.

Tighter than the rope they used to use to lynch away our identities.

I know what you must think of me.

But I was here.

I was here like footprints deeply embedded into the sand.

I was here like the red lipstick left after I kissed the back of your hand.

I am Porcelain

I was here like a love letter that was never read.

"I was here" like Beyoncé said.

When my mouth is closed, I wonder if you can still hear me speak, and even though my heart is so cold, I wonder if you still pray to GOD my soul to keep.

Even if you never return, I am so thankful for your presence.

Because of you, I am who I am; You have been my greatest lesson.

64. *Somebody Else*

The hands that touched me were always touching somebody else.

The lips you kissed me with were always kissing somebody else.

Every time you saw me, you saw somebody else.

Because there was always- somebody else.

From the tears that beat so heavily against my chest, I wondered if the memories of her face would ever be put to rest.

I wondered if these thoughts would ever simply go away.

The pain ached so deeply in my heart, yet it told me that I was strong enough to stay.

I do not quite understand, I thought we were on the same team.

I hurt you in very many ways, I know, but how could you do THIS to me?

Did you ever think for one second that the fire you lit would ignite some ether neither one of us ever could handle?

I am Porcelain

I replayed your escapades over and over again, as if they were an episode of Scandal.

What ever happened to that stop sign that you once had?

Or, could it be that you just wanted anyone more than me that damn bad?

I cannot describe the anguish; I cannot fathom the disbelief.

Your lies taunted my thoughts causing my pain to be on repeat, I repeat.

Your lies came creeping up inside of me, inside of my soul.

I kept thinking that maybe I was tripping because certain shit started getting old.

But I was telling myself the truth.

I was right in every aspect even though I lacked physical proof, until POOF everything hit the fan!

I was absolutely right!

She was your number one fan, rooting for the nonexistence of you and I, so I planned to make her pay.

I planned to painfully surprise her, all for the glory of me seeing her have a bad day; but of course, it didn't happen.

I am Porcelain

I just wanted to see her bleed, for lack of a better caption, but caption this.

A friend who really isn't a friend but a mistress, scared to call herself a side bitch, but how else do you hoes label yourself when you truly do not come first?

You're absolutely on the side.

You are supposed to be a secret; something motherfuckers are trained to hide.

But in this day and age things have changed.

Because in this generation, it's okay for the world to know a side bitch's name.

Not only is it okay to know her name, it's okay for the world to see her face.

It's okay for the wife or girlfriend to suspect such foolish mistakes.

Pure fuckery.

But everyone wants to call her crazy because when she finds out, she aims for the highest price of cutlery.

I thought I made clear in the beginning, do not fuck with me, she says.

I am Porcelain

She is in the mode to kill, kill, kill, as this information processes through her head, because she can't help but to imagine you sexing this bitch in her bed.

She can't help but imagine her rights being read because this is something that she doesn't mind doing time for, herself.

And she would love to lock you both inside of a burning building as she walks away, hearing you scream for help.

She doesn't care.

No need to be mad because it was you that brought her there.

65. AWE

I mean, how could she love ME this much?

Did my bitter broken behaviors not scare her enough?

Had I not been the failure that my roots prepared me to be?

How could she love me?

How could she strip me from all false things and still stare upon my face as though I were a Kardashian?

I keep trying to figure it out but then I get all mad again; like how could she do it?

How could she love me?

Didn't anybody tell her that I am NOT loveable?

And that all I cause is heartache?

I have verbally and physically abused her, this... is a mistake.

I subjected her to the deepest pains, ruined her.

Yet, she often smiles when she sees me.

My soul collapses upon this reality, because I thought that love was supposed to be easy.

She loves me; she's loved me for a very long time.

I am Porcelain

She paints romance across the depths of my heart.

Even when pain retracts her lines.

66. She Lost her P

They say pussy is power.

Ladies- stop giving away your pussy, I mean power.

He still won't call you tomorrow.

He still won't remember your name.

He still won't tell his wife because ain't a damn thing changed.

So, ladies- stop giving away your power, I mean pussy.

You will still feel like shit.

You will still call your best friend vowing that you are fed up with all of it.

Your power, your pussy.

Your pussy, your power.

Did you know that you are the bomb?

Did you know that lots of women paved the way for us to unapologetically belong?

We distort these journeys by subjecting ourselves to being toyed with.

I am Porcelain

We settle for second and third place as if we were a voided misfit, magically bound to bullshit.

We are more than quick fucks and bittersweet memories.

Sad thing is most of us know this, yet we fold to flesh that we could never have.

We run marathons that possess absolutely no finish line, and then we blame the other party for all the confusion.

We are aware of our demented ways.

They say pussy is power; Ladies stop giving away your pussy, stop giving away your power.

67. *When I Die*

When I die, may my burial plot be in poetry.

For it is the only place that my body has ever known.

The only place in where I truly belong.

Poetry never judged me.

Poetry looked out for me.

Poetry loves me.

The only time that it makes me cry is because its depths are tragically beautiful.

Poetry never calculated my body count and then shamed me for it.

It thrived in my name.

Poetry made me feel unconditional love.

Poetry never changed.

68. *Reminiscence*

You know that I crave your presence every time you leave.

I await your return so that I can get on my knees.

PLEASE-

Don't make me miss you.

I don't know how to control myself.

My lips want to kiss you,

I need some help... with this.

Our love burned like cigarettes and then died like cancer; how could you forget?

Crazy how things changed.

You used to love me like, I mean really love me like- I was worth all the pain.

Don't you remember?

I am Porcelain

69. <u>Angry</u>

My vagina is angry because you did not touch her today.

My vagina is angry because you did not love her today.

My vagina is angry because you didn't want to come out and play.

My vagina is angry because you made her feel this way.

My vagina is angry because you did not reach so far inside her, that you felt her heartbeat vibrating through the walls of her home.

My vagina is angry because she has been begging for your attention, but you left her alone.

She groomed herself so softly and so fine, but you missed the memo.

My vagina, my pussy, has been stuck in demo.

Mode.

Since when was fucking so hard?

Since when was raging sexual passion so far gone?

My vagina is angry.

Tell me, is she wrong?

70. *Dreaming*

It was but a dream that I remembered your face.

But a dream that you'd be right here speaking to me.

Embracing me.

Encouraging me.

It was but a dream.

That you'd be silencing me with just one look.

I fought for your attention.

Your promises.

Your compromises.

Your presence is a taste that I cannot remember.

A kiss that I will always forget.

A memory.

It was but a dream that you came to me.

71. Does it rain in the Summer?

Does it rain in the summer?

Tell me.

Does the world even cry when the sun is shining?

Does the heart of the sky break because its faith has been shaken and therefore, it's been pining... away?

Withering into the depths of storms no reporter could've ever saw coming today.

Does it rain?

Does the sunshine no longer matter if its foundation is in pain?

Would we still see those raindrops?

Those hard to see but easy to feel substances that hit you all at once.

Those feelings.

The world is...

in its feelings.

Does it rain in the summer?

I am Porcelain

Will darkness come upon us and our beautiful world cease to exist?

Or will we drown from all its had to bear from the many summers before?

I am Porcelain

72. <u>Tyler Perry</u>

My name is Brittiny.

I live in Fort Worth, Texas but I am very much familiar with the realm of greatness.

I speak encouraging affirmations with your name in it and bump music like "Win, Win, Win, Win" on my playlist.

I am looking for you.

In my everyday life, I speak your name into my future.

I am waiting for you,

I will hit the ground running; I am gunning for my place.

I have rounds of ammo ready to sound off on anyone who denies me that space; that chance.

I have talents that I could never master alone and I'm always researching ways to advance.

But truth is, I cannot afford and have not trusted anyone to represent me correctly, all I want is you.

I have experienced the scammers, the rock bottoms, and the sad, sad, truth-

that no matter how talented I am, if the right person does not lay eyes on me, I will never exist.

I am Porcelain

I decided to finally follow my heart; Tyler Perry, you're the only name on my list.

73. *Tainted*

We live in a world where predators are created when we do not speak up.

Where your friend will convince you to leave your husband,

not because he's simply a bad man, but because she is fucking him.

We live in a world.

We live in a world where women are constantly birthing babies that they will not love.

Where fathers are promising their presence to a child that they will never see again.

We live in a world.

Where depression is associated with social media.

Where dreams are broken, and people are dying.

We live in a world.

Where funerals turn into family reunions and family secrets turn into confessions.

In a world.

I am Porcelain

Where the troubled won't speak and the corrupted run the show.

In a world where your supervisor will hide your promotions, so that you will not grow.

We live in a world.

A world that will allow us to love it, but it will never love us back.

We live a world where we cannot breathe.

We are subjected to the worsts realities here, yet we never want to leave.

I am Porcelain

74. <u>MAMA</u>

I was searching for ways to find her, but my mind kept playing tug-of-war.

To be honest, I didn't quite understand exactly what I was searching for.

I just wanted to know where my mama could've been.

I wondered if my mama had been forgiven for her sins.

I wondered if my mama even had time to ask.

I wondered if my mama, was somewhere that she could laugh.

If she was enjoying herself.

I am at a loss for words, as I have been at a loss of her.

75. *Empty Flying Bullets*

A mother has to bury her child today.

There are sisters who no longer have a brother.

There are cousins who no longer have their cousin.

A best friend, whose best friend, is really gone.

There is a father who unfortunately won't make his way back home.

Tell me what did you gain from those empty flying bullets?

You forced him to leave his children, you just had to be the one to pull it; the trigger.

Society gets to see him in the star telegram, all to be viewed as just another nigga.

My soul aches when I realize how heartless the world truly is.

I can't seem to grasp the vengeance in it; a mother is left without her kid.

Tell me do you feel her pain?

Did this dramatic action reconcile what you were so very anxious to change?

I am Porcelain

Nobody deserves to be murdered; to die.

That cold blood will not resurrect his presence.

Why?

Those empty flying bullets.

What a waste of your existence, why did you have to pull it?

The trigger.

Why did you allow his death to put him down as just another nigga?

76.   *My First Love*

You raised me to be the woman that you are or the one you've always wanted to be.

You have been the illumination of my existence, the wind beneath my wings; you carried me.

From you I found guidance, I have told you my every secret.

No matter how degrading or disappointing, you've always vowed to keep it.

You are the most beautiful hat that any woman could ever wear.

In my weakest moments when I shed those tears, I remember you brushed my hair.

You mean more than the world to me.

I could never let you go.

I didn't know what GOD blessed me with, but life forced me to know.

You were always there to save me, my Angel; I am forever your little girl.

I am Porcelain

I couldn't possibly thank you enough for everything, you have changed my entire world.

Job well done.

I will say when it comes to being a Mother, YOU are the greatest one!

Happy Valentine's Day Mom.

77. <u>PAIN</u>

They never told me that pain rips your vocal cords; stops you from speaking.

I mean, takes your breath away.

They never told me that pain, leaves scars on the tissues in which once represented happiness.

How is it possible to hurt so much in one lifetime?

How is it that one could be subjected to such heartache?

I wonder.

I wonder if one knew the amount of anguish in which they'd experience, if they'd still choose to come here, to this world.

I am Porcelain

Loss is a mother, a daughter, a son, a father, an aunt, an uncle, a cousin, a best friend, a loved one; PAIN is happening.

My vocal cords are ripped.

78. _Broken Memories_

I remember when you used to "love" me.

When I could make you smile.

Your arms were my home.

The way you looked at me would take my breath away.

I remember the day that I opened my heart to you.

The day I started to love you.

I thought that you were everything.

The way you spoke and carried yourself.

It intrigued me.

The way you touched me.

It changed me.

I wanted every part of you.

I NEEDED every part of you.

But I could never have you the way that I wanted.

I could never even love you the way that I wanted.

I remember when all of my thoughts began to revolve around you.

I am Porcelain

You were in my dreams and in my thoughts; I couldn't get you out of my head.

I wanted to talk to you all day and all night.

I wanted to see you every day without having to ever tell you goodbye.

You were everything.

I remember when I started to push you away.

I never had anyone quite like you.

Nobody made me feel the way that you did.

And it scared me, you scared me.

I wish that I could have let you in.

All I wanted was to show you the real me.

The girl people have yet to meet.

But I could never do that.

I was terrified.

I was broken.

I AM broken.

I remember when you started to pull away.

I am Porcelain

It broke my heart, it broke me.

I only had myself to blame.

All you did way try.

You asked for so little, but yet and still, I gave you nothing.

I shut you out.

I remember when you stole my heart.

You reached into my chest and snatched it out effortlessly.

Taking it and everything that I had left with you.

You left me empty.

I remember when I meant something to you.

I remember when you cared.

I remember when I THOUGHT that you loved me.

Would you believe that I still love you?

I can't believe that I still love you.

I can't believe that all I have now is broken memories.

There isn't a stitch that could fix this.

No time travel to mend this.

No way for me to forget this.

I am Porcelain

For me to forget you.

I remember.

And I always will.

79. The Stutter of a Broken Child

"Get up NOW!

Didn't you hear me calling your name?"

"Mmmama, Mma I-

"Shut UP!

Just do what I told you to do!"

Straggling from bed was a boy who appeared to be normal.

His eyes were big and blue; they dared to tell a story.

Managing to stand up, he asked her-

"Ddddin't you hear me?"

He braced himself.

I am Porcelain

"I DON'T have time for this today, put your clothes on."

"I I I said- dddidn't you hear me?

I cried for you ... when Joe was here.

He he he-

"SPIT IT OUT!"

She shouts.

"He he he hurt me last night.

You you you never pay attention.

When he's here.

I can't stand up straight anymore."

80. The Ramblings of an Angry Woman

I made love to you last night.

Your skin became mine; we were permanent.

Everlasting.

On the verge to an awakening of my inner self.

I awaited your return.

The vibrations of my thighs were singing you a lullaby.

You swallowed my persuasion and tempted me to watch.

My climax was the greatest story of all.

But my peach drove you elsewhere.

You finally conquered me.

I wasn't ready.

To be subjected to the pain of losing you.

I wanted to cum… again.

I wanted our skin to become one again.

But you chose her.

Was my mouth not warm enough for you?

I am Porcelain

You tasted like the sun.

Was my tongue not wet enough?

You were a bath that I wanted to run.

81. Who am I?

I am Dirty B.

Nothing at all similar to Dirty Diana.

More like Dirty Bitch.

More like Dirty Britt.

More like Dirty; the unequivocal depths of cluttered, battered bullshit.

I am Dirty B.

Not afraid to bring the fire.

I am ether.

My words put a noose around your darkest desires.

I am truth.

I am what you are afraid to call yourself.

I am you.

I am Porcelain

82. *Face Destroyed*

Face destroyed.

Heart in pieces.

The cavity of my chest

caving

to the pits of a never- ending beginning

of my mother's nonexistence.

I was wishing

for the pain to go away.

I was wishing

that my mother would've stayed.

I prayed

but I guess that it was meant for it to be this way.

There she was

standing

but not breathing.

There she was

sleeping but not sleeping.

I am Porcelain

Kim.

Won't you please come back to me?

My life has been a mess without you.

Your body, hard as wood.

Second time I touched you-

After death.

I knew that the holes in my soul had nothing left.

I was withering.

Face destroyed.

Mind in circles.

I be tired of this pain.

I be tired of the hail every time I step OUT into the rain.

I be tired of this change.

I can never let you go.

I see your face within my face, it's such a bittersweet glow.

Face destroyed.

Memories never fading.

I am waiting.

I am Porcelain

For you.

Mama.

I am Porcelain

83. <u>WOMAN</u>

Nipples so firm, you could see them through her bra.

Ass so fat, she was stopping every car.

She was a woman.

Her curves spoke the right language.

It spoke men.

It spoke women.

It spoke

respect me-

I do not play.

Her curves-

said I've been places.

Her curves said-

I'm looking for a good time.

They said-

I drink nothing, oh nothing, but the finest of wines.

Her curves spoke-

I will not call you back tomorrow.

I am Porcelain

Her curves-

said that you are living on borrowed...

time.

She was a woman.

And damn- she, was fine.

Her smile spread like legs in mid-air.

Her laugh-

Let those bitches know that she did not care.

Her giggle-

said I'm uncomfortable, but I humor you anyway.

Her pain said yea I been hurting

but I'm okay.

She was a woman.

84. *A Missed Call*

I turned my phone on "silent."

Couldn't quite fathom the reality of a conversation

- with you.

Didn't know that it would be my last.

Ring, ring.

Ring, ring.

I didn't get to tell you that you mattered more than anything.

Ring, ring.

Ring, ring.

Didn't get to say that I'll never let anyone else come in between

-us.

So, here I lay.

Drowning in disgust.

Staring at the RED words that informed me of your missed call,

I realize that the call wasn't the only thing that I missed.

I am Porcelain

Ring, ring.

Ring, ring.

Won't you kiss me like that again?

Ring, ring.

Ring, ring.

Won't you hit me from the back again?

I was mad at you; I was mad at them.

Ring, ring.

Won't you please come back to me?

RING.

So that I may lay in your arms happily.

RING, RING.

My insides will never cave the same.

Holding onto my phone, holding onto the pain.

I missed a call from you.

85. More Truth

Alcohol and I had a bad break up.

I wanted to cry but something told me to pick my face up.

You can only cover your tears for so long behind the makeup.

Guess the ghost of a virgin girl was begging for me to wake up.

"I'll take a hoe bath in the morning."

Because the man across the room was giving me the eye, while I was pouring.

Vodka knew that home was the last place that I would be going.

But we broke up.

It was fun while it lasted.

86. *Manipulations of the Heart*

My words were powerful, but not powerful enough to bring you back to me.

When the phone calls stopped coming, life was still happening.

I've had nightmares ever since.

Ruined mentally, I physically ceased to exist.

A motherless child, I am.

Confused and hurt, I am.

Still waiting for you to appear, so that I may breathe again, I am-

Still waiting.

Is it crazy that at your funeral, I stood over your casket anticipating-

the opening of your eyes?

It's been almost 6 years, and my heart still lies-

to me.

It tricks me into believing that I have missed calls from you.

I am Porcelain

Makes me think that you are still lying in a hospital bed somewhere.

I'm still trying to figure out what happened, I just don't know.

My mind is struggling, I cannot let go.

87. *Baby Boy; The Poem*

Her tears ran like water; fast and quickly.

She said, "Jody my Jody, I thought you'd never hit me."

She was broken.

She was confused.

He had just fucked somebody else, but she was getting abused.

She hit him first you say?

Well what would you do?

How many Jodys do you have?

Did he rain on your vagina with an STD, and then get upset with YOU for being mad?

But he didn't fuck?

You're right, but he was going to.

That threat using "Daddy Dick" was simply foreplay because he had the "juice."

He was already "giving it" away.

Was that pop to the nose not worth his childish games?

He was fucking something serious.

I am Porcelain

Selling clothes to hoes but treating Yvette as though she be delirious.

That's what they do.

Use you, abuse you and pretend as though they have nothing to prove.

Jody, my Jody.

How could you treat me this way?

How could you tell me that you love me and make me feel that everything would be okay?

Jody.

I thought that you'd care for me like no other.

But as I laid crying on that couch, you only cared to run to your mother.

Did she hug you tight enough this time?

I am sick of being subjected to this bullshit and your tired ass lines.

Jody.

You don't love me no more.

I am Porcelain

I stood in the pouring rain, hoping to find a man beyond that door,

but you slammed it in my face.

I became a slave to my past when Rodney grabbed me by my waist.

I just wanted you to come home.

He tried to rape me in front of my son,

I was somewhere I didn't belong.

Without you.

Can you see me?

I'm doing just fine.

I sit here in this grass,

playing card games,

pretending that you'll do right this time.

88. *Stand*

WE *women be strong around one another, not too afraid to stare each other in the eyes to scream, to laugh, to cry.*

WE women be daring with one another; never weak to bend behind the whim of a man.

WE women,

WE women-

Be strong enough to stand.

89. Gun Violence

There were bullets with your name on em.

Bullets that pierced your soul, yea they got your pain on em.

Unidentified and to this day, I hated to see you go out like that.

Out like niggas

that were supposed to be yo niggas,

plotting behind your back.

My heart aches for your children because they never got to know you.

Yea they remember your face,

but they never got to grow with you.

To know the truth.

You crossed my mind; I know your birthday's tomorrow.

Every year on September 6, I am filled with so much sorrow.

Rest in peace, love, and bittersweet memories Kevin Hubbard #StopGunViolence

90. <u>Freedom</u>

Visions brighter than the sun.

I run.

To my freedom.

Asking for it to release my existence.

You found me bound in chains

of resistant fangs that sank into my soul.

I cried out to you the broken silence of my pain.

You trusted my instincts because you wanted me to change.

But I can't.

Face mangled with defeat;

you couldn't possibly beat what is already bent.

I'm nothing more than what you wanted me to be, and with every piece of my sanity,

I crumble.

Like notebook paper.

91. *Jesus Wept, & So Did I*

Jesus wept, and so did I.

We were remembering the look on my face, when I found out that my mother had just died.

The world knew; it was no secret.

It was blasted before I could say anything,

I wanted to keep it; the secret.

My pot broke.

And I had nothing to hold all these roots up.

Nothing to make me stand straight or talk without a lump in my throat;

I could not be tough.

She was gone.

Jesus wept, and so did I.

We were remembering the last time that she was home.

The last time that she said my name.

Jesus wept, and so did I.

I did not want my life to change.

I am Porcelain

And He knew this.

He also knew that we couldn't alter my reality, so he helped me through this.

Jesus wept, and so did I.

He saw me falling.

Drinking myself to hell; burying myself in memories of my mother,

as I was still under Death's spell.

He wept.

He told me that he was sorry that I felt all the ways that I have felt; He understands.

I told him that I appreciated it, and that I would respect GOD's plan.

92. Dear Mama

Dear Mama,

You were on my mind like yesterday.

Dear Mama,

You left me after I begged for you to stay.

Dear Mama,

Sometimes I wake up, hoping to just see you standing next to me.

Dear Mama,

This unexplainable heartache has occurred, I cannot breathe.

Dear Mama,

I'm sorry if I ever hurt you; I didn't mean it... this is true.

Dear Mama,

I've been in so much pain, I'm hurting... just like you.

Dear Mama,

I know why you were so angry and upset all the time.

Dear Mama,

I am Porcelain

I thought that you were superhuman, I thought that you'd be fine...

Dear Mama,

How could you leave me hanging? You should've said goody bye...

Dear Mama,

How do I fight back these tears?

I don't want to cry...

Dear Mama,

You stopped visiting me in my dreams...

Dear Mama,

Don't do this to me, I don't want reality to be exactly what it seems.

Rest in Peace, Love, and my Poetry, Kimberly R. Hubbard.

93. <u>Ghetto</u>

I wanted to be her.

Her,

Over there.

Becky.

Hey Becky,

Becky, with the good hair.

I don't want to be ghetto.

Don't want to be labeled the same.

Don't want to be judged, but ain't a damn thing changed.

I'm just a black girl.

Don't want them to fear me.

Don't want them to think that I won't conduct myself properly.

Can you hear me?

I don't want to be ghetto.

Don't want to be buried beneath the feet of your ego.

My skin bows down to you, but that's due to habit.

I am Porcelain

I recoil on the inside but stand proudly because I am Savage.

I continue to surpass your expectations; I am not average.

You're no better than me.

I'm no better than you, we are equal.

I will not hide behind who I am, we are just people.

94. *I'm So Dope*

I'm so dope that I inject my pain into the brains of broken daughters,

Broken fathers,

Broken mothers,

Broken husbands;

I'm so dope.

I'm so dope I take my pussy and use it as shotgun.

She be firing away like a white man who just shot one.

You know, one of us niggas.

So dope that I can tell you why they continue to pull the triggers.

They envy the audacity of us.

Our backs are too strong.

We weren't supposed to make it out of slavery, we shouldn't have lasted this long.

But, I'm so dope.

I'm so dope that I turn housewives into hoes.

I am Porcelain

They bleed novels of agony and tell me stories that nobody knows.

I'm so dope.

I'm so dope that I don't give a fuck if they sorry,

got vendettas against me,

They mad?

Well probably.

I'm so dope.

I'm so dope that I stand alone, I get high off myself.

I am an addict.

So dope that my shit,

My shit be telepathic, if you asking,

I'm so dope.

I'm so dope that I don't even make sense sometimes.

Yet you understand that I said what the fuck I said.

So dope that my words alone are a movement.

Got chills crawling up the asses of motherfuckers who really using.

I am Porcelain

I'm so dope.

I'm so dope that I could make you cum just by reading my words.

So dope that I present punishments, giving fuck boys and girls what they deserve.

I'm so dope.

I'm so dope that I wrote a book, launched it, and sold out in less than two hours.

So dope that I recognize and understand my true power.

I'm so dope.

I'm so dope that I learned how to overcome my fear of being successful.

I will make you remember my name, in the event that you are forgetful.

I am Brittiny D. Morehead,

and I

am dope

as a motherfucker.

95. *Well Played*

Her pussy smelled like a bad attitude.

It was frowning.

Angry for many reasons.

She had been judged, judged by so many because they knew her vagina was seasoned.

She got around.

She regretted the choices that she made when her parents could not be found.

But do you know what loneliness feels like?

Imagine gasping for air, you're literally not breathing.

Not even the positivity raining upon you is worth believing.

They're deceiving you.

A lot of you niggas owe her a nut back, cuz you ain't deserve that juice.

But crying is no use, because she was built for bitches like you.

When the world is quiet and the night is still, I hear you.

Breathing like the devils that you are.

I am Porcelain

Awaiting the perfect moment to get into her head.

To tell her just enough, just enough to get into her bed.

Well played.

96. *When THEY see US*

More like when WE see YOU.

More like when we see white.

More like when we see blue.

I guess you didn't know that Black Lives Matter not TOO, but PERIOD.

You are afraid of our skin; our pigment.

YOU FEAR US?

NO.

WE.

FEAR.

YOU.

You fabricate evidence and piss on our graves.

You rejoice in your wins and don't remember our names.

Some of you, that is.

Some of you have gunned us down in front of our kids.

As if we were the lions in the cages that you could not tame.

As if our lives never even mattered to you.

I am Porcelain

As IF you didn't know that we're simply imperfect, just like you.

As IF you have no remorse.

Because you're used to it.

How many Blacks did you kill today?

How many of them have you framed?

When was the last time you thought about how all of this shit needs to change?

I am Porcelain

97. <u>*Gifts*</u>

I judged her for her imaginations, but I had ones of my own.

I imagined freedom quite often, felt that it was where I belonged.

I also imagined myself dancing.

I was in the rain.

Carefree in the middle of a parking lot,

where nobody knew my name.

98.   *I'm No Mother*

I have no one to call my own.

No one to tell me that they love me until it gets on my last nerve.

Not one child to cradle in my arms,

one that I deserve.

I'm no mother.

I don't get to take pictures with someone who resembles me.

Don't get to celebrate the first of many birthdays and see them smiling; happy.

Can't hug them and wish them well at school.

Cannot educate them on bullying other kids, and how it's not cool.

I'm no mother.

I have no one to cry with.

Not one tissue that will soak up these tears.

I have no one to die with.

I am almost 30,

I am Porcelain

and I've never met you.

I've saw you in my dreams,

I would've never left you.

For the first time is 8 years,

I've accepted this heartache like no other.

No matter how many sympathy messages I receive,

I am no child's mother.

99. <u>Beauty</u>

Your eyes are mountains rising to the occasion;

they are infectious.

I dared to understand what was behind them.

It's as though I am staring at a canvas,

enveloping the depths of beauty at its finest;

I am smitten.

100. ATTENTION

STOP what you're doing and fuck me.

Thought I'd make you cum twice so that you would love me.

Showed you my vulnerable side, so that you will hug me.

But in the end,

You still made me feel ugly.

Figured if you bragged on me enough, I'd feel lucky.

I was wrong.

Your compliments stung like poison; odd and strong.

I didn't understand.

How could I have become the very thing that recoiled from your hands?

I am Porcelain

101. *Judge Me Not*

Do you ever pet dogs that you meet outside?

Do you hold them?

Do you let them lick you, and rest their paws across your shoulders?

Well, people are like dogs;

we love them, until we know where they've been.

Don't me get wrong,

I was just a fuck to some but eventually,

I did the fucking,

because somebody had me fucked up.

This mentality was problem, but I could not fix it.

I became a man with a vagina;

I just wanted them to listen-

to me.

102. She Swallows

Women have been dealing with shit for years.

Yet they persevere, as if the world isn't watching.

Waiting for them to fall.

To fail.

To fuck up.

The world is always waiting.

But she swallows.

She allows the course of pain to rush down her throat, as she waits for tomorrow.

Praying for better circumstances.

Wishing that someone would bless her enough, so that she may feed her children today.

Grieving the loss of her husband.

She continues to swallow.

Awaiting the response from a good job on time that isn't borrowed.

She doesn't have anything, but she tries anyway.

She cleans houses and babysits for little to no pay.

I am Porcelain

What a hard pill.

She spent the last two weeks selling herself because she couldn't afford to pay the bills.

She swallowed.

Her new boyfriend doesn't help, and he hits her sometimes.

She stands up after getting her ass beat and pretends that everything is all fine.

She cooks him dinner.

She goes above and beyond, just so that he will remember-

her.

103. Withered

If this love were a flower, it would shrivel up and die.

I waited for you to love me correctly, but after so many years, why try?

I kept convincing myself that you were the one for me.

That you'd marry me soon.

Thirteen years later, when you finally proposed;

I was the only fool in the room.

I said yes, when I knew that you were in love with somebody else.

But somehow, I managed to manipulate the truth because I wanted happiness for myself.

Two years later, you're still yearning for her.

Was it worth it?

I found out that you had her in my bed,

so, I killed you both on purpose.

I am Porcelain

104. <u>Something about the way that she ate my pussy</u>

Her pussy was breathing on my neck.

We were doing 69, you know 69.

I will never forget.

Out of respect,

I will spare you the details.

But I would like to paint you a picture as to where my thoughts sail.

I remember the day that she reached into my soul.

Her fingers caressed my walls,

she found secrets that were never told.

Like- how to make cum harder than I ever had before.

It was like the series, Locke and Key; a surprise behind every door.

There were doors to my pussy.

My legs were numb, it was so gushy.

I couldn't believe it.

I am Porcelain

I was in another world.

I had been had,

and it was all by a girl.

105. *For the Big Girls*

"Oh, she must like em big."

No bitch, she likes them beautiful.

So, never mind my belly, I am simply pregnant-

with opportunity.

You are infatuated with my presence, so much so, that you still speak on me-

when I leave the room.

"She don't turn them heads like she used to."

I'm so sorry that you assumed.

You have mistaken plus size for the amount of confidence that I must lack.

What you fail to understand is that my energy, my energy matches the widest parts of my back.

Honey, you tried it.

I could have any man that you have, no matter how often your judgements deny it;

I wear my weight well.

I am a sexual beast and naturally freaky as hell.

I am Porcelain

I am the "clout," the "come-up," and the "gang, gang, gang."

So, thank you for allowing me to witness your insecurities when you mention my name.

I'm in love with who I am, now's about time we got even.

There was a man in my DM last week; Isn't your husband's name Steven?

I like to respect boundaries, but this poem is for the big girls.

I said I like to respect boundaries, but THIS poem- is for the big girls.

Let's get back to Steven.

He was sending me all sorts of messages, as IF I had to give him a reason.

I recall you spreading rumors about my stretch marks.

Funny thing is, your husband rubbed on them when he took my panties off.

Just because a woman with a little more, embraces her body, it doesn't mean that she's not trying to fix it.

I am Porcelain

The only fact of the matter is, it is none of your damn business.

I am Porcelain

106. <u>GREEN BOXES</u>

After almost 15 years of passing up the green boxes before me,

I decided to do something differently.

I wanted to sit up there again.

Wanted to feel the wind caressing my hair; my innocence.

But there was a problem.

I had gained so much weight since middle school.

The voices in my head told me that I would never be able to-

raise myself up high enough to sit there, like I used to.

I reminded that voice that I, I do what I choose to.

If I get hurt, I get hurt.

I failed my first attempt for what it is worth.

I attempted to lift myself up with a small jump.

I tried again.

I didn't want to give up because I had some shit to mend.

I am Porcelain

I failed.

I tried again immediately after, but I rose my leg this time.

My ass was high in the air for all the neighbors to see.

But I was on top, and I was fucking happy.

I positioned myself correctly.

I sat down, swinging my legs; I was ready.

The little girl in me was screaming "YES bitch!"

She was waiting for all of her friends to show up too.

She wanted to talk about what happened yesterday.

About how many boys and girls liked her.

About how sex was interesting.

About how life was going to change soon.

About how her parents had broken up.

About how life was so damn tough.

She wanted to talk.

To her past.

But she knew the reality of this Green Box would not last.

I am Porcelain

107. <u>*Free My Pussy*</u>

When you get tired of being a good girl, you know where to find me; here.

Drenched in the fluids that you left me in the first time.

I'll be here.

But when you show up, I want to fuck you in the air, so that when my soul is taken by your tongue, I'll be even closer to GOD.

Bear with me.

The troubled don't usually speak, but you my friend, will be speaking.

You see, I'm used to knocking back niggas like patron shots.

100 bottles of kinky and a lot of mouth is what I've got.

I am Sexually Awoken, but my pussy is still intact.

And I am ready, so ready to give you all of that.

Guys were like amazon products for me; I'd try them for 30 days and then return them.

I was no longer amazed by their games because I had learned them.

I am Porcelain

The walls of my vagina cave at the mere thought of your fingers crawling, reaching, tugging inside me.

I can't help but to imagine my scream, it was not worth hiding.

I remember that feeling, it felt so good.

Our clits grinding against one another, the sensitivity was understood.

So come and free me.

Masturbation is therapeutic, but you're not making this easy.

I'll be here.

Waiting for you to stand firmly behind me, whispering into my ear, -

politely, asking me if I want it.

I want to go ahead and let you know that I do.

108. <u>BIG</u>

You say you like the way that I keep myself together, for a big girl.

You told me that weight loss doesn't really take forever, even for a big girl.

You said losing thirty pounds would be good for me, because I'm a big Girl.

You tear me down and then say, "but, you're not ugly, for a big girl."

You say that my pussy is only so good because my stomach is fat.

Big Girl.

What makes you really think that I like being called that?

Big Girl.

Since when was it okay to shame someone publicly?

Do you think that I don't notice your jabs because you sound so bubbly?

I am not your Big Girl.

I was never Big Sexy.

I am Porcelain

And I wouldn't fuck you out of pity for myself, even if you let me.

But, let me make something clear.

All of your inside jokes about "big girls," they stop here.

109. You a Poet?

You a Poet?

But I ain't seen nothing from you-

Ain't heard nothing from you lately-

But you a Poet?

I thought that you would've made more noise than that by now.

Would've beat down the world with your heart by now.

Would've put a stop to violence and hate by now.

But you a Poet?

I thought you were a Poet.

I thought I saw you on the biggest stage, projecting your rage, and channeling your peace.

Thought I saw you giving hope to the streets,

But you a Poet?

You not a Poet.

You're not out there showing them what you're really made of.

Not giving them that raw truth that they crave for.

I am Porcelain

You are not a Poet.

I think you're confused.

I think you've mistaken the definition.

I think you've been used.

You're not a Poet.

You're just pretending to be.

I thought you were a Poet, stop pretending to me.

Thought I saw you crying.

Saw you fading into the background, tell me why are you lying?

You are not a fucking Poet.

You've been gone for so long, I bet you didn't even know it.

Have I torn you down enough yet?

Because you've failed, tremendously.

You've diminished all known value to self, in its entirety.

You ain't no Poet.

You're just pretending to be.

I thought you were a Poet, stop pretending to me.

I am Porcelain

Thought that you would've made more noise than that by now.

Would've beat down the world with your heart by now.

Would've put a stop to violence and hate by now.

But you a Poet?

I thought you were a Poet.

You've been gone for so long, I bet you didn't even know it.

I am Porcelain

I am Porcelain; The Naked Truth

Not enough truth yet.

I am Porcelain

One More Story

I am Porcelain

Before you go, I have one more truth to share.

In the midst of being reckless, I also contracted Gonorrhea. How did I do that? Well I was on my spree of doing anything for the right amount of money. Now sure, prior to this, I had participated in intercourse for a few things, but this transaction had gone all wrong. First and foremost, we met online. Secondly, he walked me to a vacant apartment. The price on my vagina was $3,000 for the moment. He didn't even have a room or a car... I should've known better, but I proceeded anyway; thinking that maybe it's not as bad as it seems.

Now, he had been harassing me for a while, saying that he would "pay for it" after being shot down several times by me through messages online. He was from New Orleans, said that he'd be in town for a few days on tour with a celebrity. Young and dumb, I believed him. I had good reasons for wanting the money, but it wasn't worth the degrading experience.

Entering the vacant apartment, it was hot. I should've gone home, but I needed the money. We went to the center of the floor; he pulled his pants down. It was the smallest

I am Porcelain

penis that I had ever saw, which made me think, okay, well this is why he's paying for sex. I proceeded. I began to perform oral sex, which is hard to accomplish with a penis the size of an atom. YUCK. I then began to straddle him so that I could ride him and simply make him cum, so that I could leave. It was too small. I then got on all fours. Still too small, but somehow it worked for him. Whatever.

I was wet. Like in a weird way; something just didn't seem right. He finished. I got up and went to the bathroom, can't recall if I wiped up or not because this was almost 10 years ago, but I tried my best to get the hell of there. When I tried to meet up with him later that night, he told me that I'd have to come and bail him out of jail because the police found drugs on him when he was coming out of the apartments.

Now wait a damn minute. Nothing added up.

So, you mean to tell me that I was fucked AND I got fucked?

I ignored his messages because one, I wouldn't be going to anyone's jailhouse to bail out anyone. Two, as I stated, something just was not right at all. I tried to put this in the

I am Porcelain

back of mind after it happened because I felt like such a nasty prostitute- who wasn't even a prostitute because she didn't get paid. It gets worse though.

I knew that sex with him was weird, but I thought that it was weird because his penis was a stomp, not because he was releasing his disgusting ass fluids upon me. How did I find out?

I was on the phone with a guy friend and I told him what happened. I was coughing in spurts throughout our conversation.
He was like "That nigga gave you something."
I was like "Uhm don't say that, no he didn't."
I laughed him off the phone.
Now within that week of me sleeping with shrivel-dick Willie, my ex called me. He and I had been broken up for some time. I had moved out, was mad about something. He got me to come back over. Said that he wanted to eat and watch movies. I was fine with that. At no surprise- we had sex too. It was that same weird, wet feeling that I referred to earlier. After we finished, I went home the next day or so.

Not even a week passed, my ex called me again.

I am Porcelain

He asked me if I had sex with anyone besides him. Again, we had been broken up for some time, so with an attitude I was like "Yea, why." He responded, "That nigga nasty, he gave you something."

My face was fucked. My heart sank into my vagina.

I apologized repeatedly. He didn't curse me, bash me, or anything of the sort. He said, "I'm going to take you to the clinic."

I went into the living room and told my mother and grandmother what I had done. My mother said, "Your life is like a movie." We laughed but this shit was serious, and it was certainly not funny. My grandmother's response was her classic, "Brittiny, why did you do that?" I was at a loss for words, because WHY DID I DO THIS?

So, he came over. I stood in the door of my grandmother's home with a still face. I looked him in the eyes and said "I know. I'm dirty. I'm a nasty bitch. A whore. Go ahead and say it." He reiterated that he wouldn't say those things to me. I felt even worse. He told me what he experienced and how he knew that something was wrong. I didn't have any

I am Porcelain

discharge or discoloration, but he did. I was mortified. I reverted back to shrivel-dick Willie. His name was not Willie. I don't even remember his name to be honest. I started to inform him, but I gathered that his dirty ass knew that he had it already. I was also hoping that he would give it to the wrong woman so that she'd kill him on my behalf. Like seriously, how could a penis so small release such poison?

My ex paid for my medication. They treated my mouth and vaginal area. How stupid could I have possibly been? I shook my head the entire time. His meds were more expensive than mine, which made me feel even worse.

How could I have done this to someone? I judged women who did shit like this. Now, I was the slut; how ironic.

He said that he wanted me to come back to what was our home. I stayed there with him while we both took our medications for this STD. I couldn't stop apologizing. He never threw it in my face, even after we got back together. Yes, we got back together, crazy as it sounds. While taking our meds with no sex involved, we were able to connect differently.

I am Porcelain

I had never encountered this type of respect before. I hope that somewhere somebody's daughter has this same love when they make a mistake, because we all certainly make mistakes.

So, to you, my reader, be mindful of what you do to AND with your body.

Be careful with the situations that you put yourself in.

And if you ever have to have sex for money, GET THE MONEY FIRST!!! (LOL).

No, seriously. Your body is truly a temple. I never realized that but it's sacred and should be respected at all times.

These men do not deserve to abuse it or you. Please remember that in every moment moving forward. Reverting back to when I was raped, I recall the first red flag that should have made me run and it wasn't the porn; it was when he made me let him stick his dick in me to see if I had been cheating. It was disgusting and degrading but I submitted out of fear and this obligation that sat in my stomach. I had not cheated on him, yet I allowed him to embarrass me in this way. We must learn to stand up

I am Porcelain

for ourselves better because shit like THAT is truly unacceptable.

Contracting gonorrhea was hard for me to share because the backstory is one of the most degrading memories of my past, but it is necessary for me to share because something so simple almost ruined my life. It could have been AIDS. I judged girls for doing what I did, until it was me.

We will not end in sadness dwelling on our pasts, we will end in happiness for overcoming our secrets and our flaws. Sometimes you must say everything out loud in order to feel the truth within yourself, so that you can assess it, and fix it. I hope that the fear of my experiences make you feel UNcomfortable enough to do so too.

I am Porcelain

I am Porcelain; The Naked Truth

Not a one-hit-wonder.

I am Porcelain

The Naked Truth is the first version of this book; I created it based on wanting to simply publish a book of poetry. Along the way, with encouragement from my stepmother, it became much more than that.

I'm not sure if it was her own curiosity, or the fact that she's an English teacher that made her push me, but she suggested that I tell my fans what brought me to exhibit such poetry.

I took the challenge and decided to *undress myself* for the world. This was 9 years ago.

I rushed through my book due to the nervousness of my mother's health; I wanted her to see me step into my dream. I needed her to know that I could do it because when she became ill, she doubted everything, *including me.*

She finally got to hold my book in her hands before she passed away, but she never got the chance to read it. It always bothered me that she didn't get to know my truths as her daughter, but I realize now that she and I have the same story, *because she was a Broken Daughter too.*

I wanted so badly to fix her pain, but I couldn't. My only

regret now is that we didn't heal together.

The very first copy that I received as a Published Author, she held. When she was cremated, I placed it with her, hoping that she would hear the story that I ached so badly for her to know.

I shared a lot of my life in the first version, but as the years passed, I saw many things that I wish I had done differently; so, I decided to revamp it because I am a firm believer in satisfying my desires/thoughts. I needed to share more.

The Naked Truth did wonderful in sales and touched the hearts of many. On the next few pages, you are welcomed to dive into the feedback from readers on Amazon and Social Media.

Thank you.

Reviews from Amazon

⇒ **Frank Baez-** *"Must read!!! This book is not only a book, it's pages full of heart and soul, so much effort put in, YOU HAVE TO READ THIS BOOK!!!"*

⇒ **Timothy Roth** - *"Wildly impressive for what you would never expect. I know the author. Personal friend of mine. And when she told me she wrote this book, I laughed because I didn't think she was serious. I wasn't expecting what I read. It will put you to tears, wanting hugs, opening your eyes to things you'd never fathom if they weren't right in front of you."*

⇒ **Yoama Vera-** *"Amazing. I couldn't put the book down! I was in tears reading this, very inspirational. Took me 2 days to read the entire book."*

I am Porcelain

⇒ **Venus Parmes-** *"Very good read. I've never been into poetry, there are some amazing poems in the book. Definitely a must read."*

⇒ **Raychelle Meyers-** *"Awesome Poetry!"*

⇒ **Unknown -** *"Definitely worth the buy and read; Phenomenal."*

⇒ **Xena-** *"It seems true to life, brought back memories."*

⇒ **Grandma's Left Arm-** *"An innovation to poetry; so much truth in the poems. Read this and you will heal with the Author."*

Reviews from Social Media

⇒ *Janice Majors-* "Omg where do I start with this review!!! Being that I've read it over 4 times I'd say it's my favorite book!!! You find yourself getting so lost in the pages that you imagine yourself in the very moment as Brittiny!!! Some of the pages made me cry, some made me let out a belly aching laugh, and then there were those pages where secretly you close your eyes and moan. I recommend this book to every girl running from something, or needing something to escape away from for a sec. The author is talented beyond words, she's brilliant with her words."

⇒ *Shantea Smith-* "I love how you put your heart and soul in The Naked Truth. You didn't hold nothing back. I love it girl, so many tears while reading it."

⇒ *Jasmine Baker-* "Book was brutally amazing. Never seen a person have such a raw connection

I am Porcelain

between the pen and paper. It's almost as if the pen was connected to her and the emotions literally just flowed through. Her spoken words were a barrel filled with unspoken thoughts, fears, worries, and trauma of others, and she cracked it all open. She didn't step into a platform, she made one of her own. I can only imagine the fan base and supporters she gained just from them simply feeling as if their story was finally being told. She is an Author that's definitely worth keeping an eye on because she's only going to level up from here. She doesn't just do this.... she IS this!"

⇒ **Hillary Parker-** *"The Naked Truth? Oh, it was definitely that. The hardcore truth from the depths of her soul, or at least that's what it felt like. Even if you haven't experienced what she spoke of, you felt it! You could feel everything she was saying as if you were the one with the pen and paper in your hand. A lot of people may not have the guts to express the things that she expressed. Neither do they have the talent to put rhythm behind it. It was truly an amazing read.*

Brittiny stood up for a lot of women with this one. I can only imagine what the revamped version will be like. Get ready for your hearts to flutter because she's truly a talented one when it comes to this! I love it!"

⇒ **Mark Johnson-** *I loved this book!!!! The poems really let you know her story and I loved the poem dedicated to me.*

⇒ **Nessa Brown-** *"Hell, it made it to the English Dept at the school where I work! My coworker only got 1 copy and it's in my classroom. When the office aide brought it to me, two girls in my custody could not put it down; they sat next to each other and read various pages. They wanted to take it with them. Love how you didn't hold back on anything. You did a great job cuz!"*

⇒ **Nisha-** *"Why does He? - is the best poem; it spoke to me. Your drive and success inspired me to write a poem of my own."*

⇒ **Olivia Rolland-** *"I'm on page 47 and I LOVE it already!!! Brittiny, you have outdone yourself Ms. Lady!!!"*

⇒ **Celeste Hindman-** *This is my favorite book; I will always support you Sis!"*

⇒ **Qualonda D. Wright-** *"My little cousin has written a book and I am so proud of her!"*

⇒ **Vanessa Belton-** *"She's such a beautiful young Author! So very proud of you Brittiny!"*

⇒ **William Washington-** *"I had the pleasure of being part of this project. It is a collection of incredible poems, check it out!"*

⇒ **Anthony Depree-** *"Got to show support! Grab a copy online with Barnes & Noble!"*

⇒ **Bionka Morehead-** *"My twin is better than yours, she's an Author and a Poet!!"*

⇒ **Kandace Matheus-** *"Don't sleep on this… IF YOU DON'T HAVE THIS IN YOUR LIFE, COP YOU ONE! I PROMISE YOU WON'T BE DISAPPOINTED!!!"*

⇒ **Danielle Luna-** *"I read a little so far, it really touched me, you're such a great writer! I hope GOD blesses you with many more blessings."*

⇒ **Mackenzie Linzy-** *"It was awesome! Loved every poem, such a great way to get to know a beautiful person. The range of poems are amazing, from Family, Self-Love, and Personal Struggles, it's a great read; I have read it multiple times. Brittiny you are such a great writer; I'm honored to call you my friend. I would definitely recommend this to anyone who is into reading because it's THAT DAMN GOOD, ha!"*

⇒ **Misty Lemon-** *"I can't wait to read the next one, girl you are an amazing person and a blessing to many."*

I am Porcelain

⇒ **Krissy Evans-** *"This was more than a book of poetry. It was a truth of unspoken words from most women who are scared to speak out. It's feelings of which I can relate, a real damn... I felt that moment, I've read it at least four times. It's one of my favorites to grab with a glass of wine."*

⇒ **Bj Williams-** *"This book though- RELEVANT. "Sometimes I choke in my sleep due to the inability to swim... far away." Quoted from the Jasmine Mans Poem; No lie, I cried like a baby when I heard the recorded version of it on YouTube."*

⇒ **Raychelle Meyers-** *"This book is ruthless! I love how the Author captures your attention, right from the start. She's the real deal and I absolutely love this book. A Must Read Indeed!"*

⇒ **Netoi M. Sheridan-** *"At this airport VEGAS BOUND and brought some reading material, tell me why this girl Brittiny has me here teary-*

eyed. ("So, I decided to look hatred in the face. I no longer feel dishonor or disgrace my mistakes. I've been asleep for so long, but now, I'm wide awake.") I am so extremely proud of the woman you're becoming. Your book is awesome, love you beautiful!"

⇒ **Portlan Tune-** *"So lots of people own this book by now. I was late getting mine, but I've heard the best is saved for last! Not only do I have a brilliant friend that is an Author and Poet, I got her copy with tattered pages, makeup, and perfume! So proud to own the copy Brittiny once carried with her. OOwee this story has more to tell."*

⇒ **Porsche Hines-** *"My boo about to blowwwww up!!"*

⇒ **Nicole Hunter-** *"I finally got my copy; I've read a bit and I can't wait to finish reading it. I pray that all of your dreams and ambitions come true honey."*

⇒ **Chandra Franklin-** *"Baby, your manager, (that white man) couldn't believe what the hell he was seeing himself! Came around the corner looking like shiiiittt is she ONLY SELLING BOOKS?!!!"*

⇒ **Daniele D. Morehead-** *"My daughter, your words are like razors, they cut clean to the bone; I like it."*

⇒ **Erica Darden-** *"It's only a matter of time before your fans are selling your wigs on Amazon and eBay."*

⇒ **Linda Washington-** *"This is why I love you, because you love me. Kim would so proud. I remember when you were little and you clung to me, it's still that way. We are both proud of you, you are amazing and so is this book."*

⇒ **La'Shawnda Bonner-** *"Your work is something spectacular!! Makes the hair on my arms stand up!!"*

I am Porcelain

Wise Words from Me to You

"Never put anyone's dream above your own."

"Sometimes being the coldest Savage is keeping your mouth closed and letting that shit ride; It'll play out the way that it needs to, WITHOUT you having to intervene."

"Sometimes you don't have to be the best, you just have to be good enough."

"You cannot force friendships that aren't meant to exist."

"You can never recover from a storm that has passed when you are still searching for the clouds that caused the hail in the first place; move on."

"Sometimes we must get away… from ourselves."

I am Porcelain

"You can tell when you're not living; the air suffocating your throat starts to feel like a warm hug, and the thoughts that dwell within your mind become faint, as if they're gasping for air too."

"You're so quick to claim big money, new houses, and great jobs. Claim that heartache, that failure, and that pain too, because there is clarity in it all."

"The GREAT thing about being an Author is that YOU get to choose when you will finish writing your book. The BAD thing about being an Author is that YOU CHOOSE WHEN YOU WILL FINISH WRITING YOUR BOOK. STOP BS'N AND FINISH IT, I'm proud of you already!"

"Acknowledge the value of your pussy first because it's priceless."

"Success ain't lit without a little negativity. Thank you for NOT believing in me, because I made it anyway."

I am Porcelain

"I know I'm going to be somebody; I just can't be her today."

"I may not be your choice, but I am for damn sure your voice."

"Eventually everything gets used; vaginas, books, knowledge, and cars. The goal is to handle them all with care when they are presented/given to you."

"People are like dogs; we love them until we know where they've been."

"The stature of my fame does not validate whether or not my voice is meant to be heard; my words are valuable."

"Do not be upset with me because I will not inconvenience my life for you."

I am Porcelain

"Do not use GOD to justify the matters of your bullshit. Own your mistakes because GOD has nothing to do with that."

"If you're afraid to live, then you're already dead."

"We can't be given a world that we are so bound to burn up."

"Without freedom, one is only a ruthless, wild, and rebellious animal, in which cannot be tamed; free yourselves and free others."

"Men do not define us."

"You can only be bothered when you give someone permission to fuck with your energy; to indulge is a choice. Are you choosing yourself? If not, then you should."

I am Porcelain

"I <u>honor</u> you for what you say in my face, but I <u>value</u> you for what you say behind my back."

"Live WITH purpose, ON purpose."

"The windows to our souls rely on the capabilities of apologizing and meaning it; show yourselves."

"Being imperfect does not validate fuck-boy or fuck-girl behavior."

"It IS your responsibility how people perceive you."

"Don't lose yourself trying to use yourself."

"Wisdom isn't born within; it manifests through years of ignorance."

I am Porcelain

"Having the attitude of entitlement will land you flat on your ass; to be alive isn't even promised. What makes you think that you're owed anything? The trials that we experience are a given as humans, they do not define what we deserve. We must go after what we want and in return, hope that GOD will bless us to carry out our plans. Life unfortunately has shown me that even after shooting for the stars, you can still only be handed the grass from forest fires."

"The shit isn't easy, and it hurts often, but happiness dwells within the honesty that we give ourselves."

"The first step to BEING okay is BELIEVING that you are."

"It amazes me how we're granted freedom because we tamper with it daily. Whether the chains are mental or physical; set yourself free."

I am Porcelain

"Sometimes we auction off pieces of ourselves that can't be bought."

I am Porcelain

Motivation

TRUTH MOMENT:

In the midst of writing my first book, I went into a very popular bookstore and spoke with someone about placing THE NAKED TRUTH on their shelves.

I informed her that I wasn't finished with it yet but was attempting to orchestrate a plan for when I launch it.

I guess she smelled bullshit because she looked me up and down, as if I were a walking disease, like "Girl you ain't about to write no damn book."

She asked me for my age, I was 22 years old at that time, so I told her 22.

I smile when I'm nervous, so I smiled; she just kept staring at me. This was her time to respond because I had already politely and professionally, asked my question.

I then let her know the title and the concept of my book, the direction that I have for it, etc.

iBleedPoetry

I am Porcelain

She finally provided me with a response, but she never let go of her stank energy.

How did I know that she was being "stank" towards me?

Well because a guy came into the store during this awkward conversation of ours, and she lit up all over, was suddenly friendly AND conversational. How cute right? Not so much to me. However, I continued to be polite after he left.

I took the information from her and returned a few months later after my book launched. The same woman was there. She immediately recognized me, and she did not look happy. I showed her my book; her energy changed.

I recall being extremely upset after our initial encounter, because after I left her store, I visited the one right next to it; both black owned and BOTH owners were horrible to me. What the fuck right?

I am Porcelain

I went to my car in tears. I was young, trying to find my way or follow a road that may have been paved for Young Authors like me, but I was at a dead end that day.

As I stated, when I returned and placed my book into her hands, her energy shifted. I saw a smile, and I gained a conversation from her. A handful of my books were featured on their shelves and they sold out quickly. I never returned. THE NAKED TRUTH continued to thrive.

No matter how you are treated along the way, "POP YO SHIT," as they say in this generation.

What you bring to any table matters. Remember that and remember me.

Brittiny D. Morehead

What's Next?

<u>The Art of Words</u> is next; it was mastered in a Creative Writing course Brittiny attended at a community college. As a student, she was responsible for compiling and creating a book of short stories. Due to her love for the *art of words,* she did more than just that; these short stories are only the beginning of many novels to come.

Also . . .

<u>Bruises of a Lover's Fist</u> will follow this release; it is the first novel Brittiny ever began to write. She began to dabble with it at 17-years-old. The first few sentences came to her when her boyfriend at the time, came home at 2am, panting like a puppy dog. When she decided where she wanted this story to go, it became a masterpiece.

What would you do with your cheating husband after he raped your 10-year daughter and then killed you six years later? *You haunt him until your soul is no longer tired.* Stay tuned.

I am Porcelain

Again, I thank you for supporting me throughout this journey; it has been a tremendous honor to have your ear.

I am Porcelain

Reflections

I am Porcelain

Reflections

I am Porcelain

Reflections

www.ingramcontent.com/pod-product-compliance
Lightning Source LLC
Chambersburg PA
CBHW020859080526
44589CB00011B/366